Healing Hidden Wounds

Healing Hidden Wounds

By Tom Klaus

Loveland, Colorado

Healing Hidden Wounds

All the stories in this book are true. For the sake of privacy, names and details have been sufficiently changed to make them unidentifiable.

Credits
Edited by Eugene C. Roehlkepartain
Book and Cover Design by Judy Atwood Bienick
Cover Photo by Jeff Buehler

Scripture quotations are from the Holy Bible, New International Version. Copyright © 1973, 1978, 1984 International Bible Society. Used by permission of Zondervan Bible Publishers.

Library of Congress Cataloging-in-Publication Data
Klaus, Tom, 1954-
    Healing hidden wounds / by Tom Klaus.
      p.   cm.
    Includes bibliographical references.
    ISBN 0-931529-70-0
    1. Church work with children of alcoholics. 2. Church work with teenagers.
3. Teenagers—Pastoral counseling of. 4. Children of alcoholics—Pastoral
counseling of. 5. Church work with problem families.   I. Title.
BV4463.7.K42 1989
261.8'322923—dc20   89-37536
                                          CIP

Printed in the United States of America

Dedication

"If I did not believe that no alcoholic who dies drunk dies in vain, then my whole life as a priest is a waste and the whole concept of the brotherhood of man is a joke. I just believe that those who die drunk have bought sobriety for the rest of us."
Father Martin

*In the spirit of these words,
I dedicate this book
to the memory of C.C. "Tom" Klaus, my dad.*

Contents

Appendixes

Acknowledgments

S itting at my desk, it's easy to believe I'm the sole con-
tributor to this book. Yet that thought is only an illusion
created by the hypnotic blinking of my computer's cursor.
In fact, there have been many contributors.

Perhaps the most material comes from numerous recovering victims of alcoholism who've shared their stories with
me for this book. The names and life details of these survivors have been changed to protect their anonymity. Nonetheless it took a lot of courage for each to speak so candidly.
A common sentiment was, "If it might help another child,
you can have my story."

I owe a tremendous debt to these worthy, honest people. Many are members of the Adult Children of Alcoholic
support groups I've attended in recent years. Thank you,
friends.

Among the others who deserve recognition for their
unique roles in the development of this book are: Joani
Schultz, who was the first to suggest it needed to be written; Marcella Ward and Brent Bill, who helped me believe in
my ability to write it; and Arlene Wheaton and Del Cop-
pinger for their consistent encouragement.

I am especially indebted to five friends who devoted
valuable time to critique my manuscript. Judy Brutz, Dave
Lewis, Pat Selburg-Smith, Royce Frazier and Nancy Pedersen
each gave me their invaluable gifts of sharp insight and
honest, fair criticism. The book is better for their unique
contributions.

Happily, Gene Roehlkepartain has been my editor at
Group Books. Since our first contact, I've been impressed
with his sensitivity to the book's content and with his note-

worthy ability. The impact of his excellent ideas, suggestions and talent for writing are visible throughout the text. Every first-time writer should be so fortunate to work with Gene.

Finally, none have contributed as greatly as my family. My wife and son are noted *not* for what they've done, but for who they are. Lynne and Jake are two amazing people who know better than any others what it is to live with me in sickness and recovery. I sincerely love them for this.

Making a Difference

Not long ago, an acquaintance asked me to describe my current passion in life. I described my concern that the church help the victims of alcoholism within its congregations and communities. Then I asked what his church was doing for this hidden population. His answer impaled my heart: "We forbid drinking and teach against it. So it's not really a problem for us."

Unlike my colleague, I believe our churches have many teenagers from alcoholic and other addictive families— whether we officially condemn or condone drinking. And I believe we haven't been effective in helping them. As a result, these young people live in pain and usually grow up to form destructive relationships and lifestyles. And they usually leave the church.

Healing Hidden Wounds describes how you can help.

Overview of the Book

You don't have to be a professional or a victim to help kids from alcoholic families. Any caring youth worker can do much for children of alcoholics. But you need to understand the difference between efforts that help and those that don't.

Healing Hidden Wounds builds a foundation for an effective, helpful ministry. I hope you'll see this book as a primer to which you will repeatedly refer in your quest to establish an effective ministry to teenagers from alcoholic families. It includes:

● the needs and concerns of alcoholic families, including discussions of the nature of alcoholism, family dynamics and roles teenagers play;

● the church's record and role in helping these families;

● practical ways to minister to teenagers from alcoholic families; and

● the struggles and needs of youth ministers who are themselves children of alcoholics.

Every chapter includes a Work It Out section. Each provides questions for thinking through and suggestions for applying the chapter's ideas. Use these sections for individual or group study.

In some instances Work It Out asks you to consider personal issues. If you're studying in a group, protect each other by establishing rules of confidentiality. Share as openly as you can, but first be true to your own perceptions and feelings.

Unless a study group maintains confidentiality, it may not be the safest place to talk about these personal issues. If you feel a need to discuss intimate concerns, seek an appropriate person and setting. Remember, those who give the best help don't hesitate to seek help when they need it.

A Personal Journey

My personal interest in children of alcoholism grows out of my own experience as a child of an alcoholic. Until after my dad died, I was never aware of how his addiction affected me and my relationships.

Early one Sunday morning in 1981, my wife and I received an emotional phone call from home. Through her sobs, my sister told me Dad had become ill in the night and had been taken to the hospital.

The next few days Dad's condition worsened rapidly. His doctor discovered an aneurysm—a burst artery—in Dad's brain. It caused a paralysis that became nearly total within days.

One week later, Dad died. He was 69.

Four years later, I learned the real cause of Dad's death.

I was attending a lecture about the medical consequences of alcoholism. At one point the speaker rattled off a list of physical problems created by chronic alcoholism: liver disease, hepatitis, cirrhosis and fetal alcohol syndrome. When she described how prolonged use of alcohol could weaken blood vessels, I began making connections.

I described my Dad's final illness, and asked if alcoholism could have caused his burst artery. She confirmed my fear.

Today I know an aneurysm only triggered Dad's death. Alcoholism was the cause.

My dad's death propelled me onto a long, painful journey. Through it, I eventually faced the impact Dad's addiction had on me. I didn't like what I found. I began to feel angry that so much of my life was spent under the influence of alcoholism. And no one—not even the church—helped me.

I hope this book will be a catalyst for healing for your youth group members who may be living in the pain of alcoholic families. Through your ministry, these wounded young people can experience God's grace and healing.

PART 1

Understanding the Pain

CHAPTER 1

The Hidden Need

A Prevalent Problem You Never See

Jerry was the ideal youth group member—friendly, outgoing, helpful, always responsible with assignments.

But Jerry worried too much. He worried about trivialities. He worried about things that weren't his responsibility. He even called the adult leaders to make sure they were ready for the next meeting.

The youth leaders dismissed Jerry's behavior as a weird quirk he'd outgrow. They never considered that it might indicate deeper problems. But the leaders weren't to blame—Jerry attended meetings incognito. He even fooled himself.

It took nearly 15 years for Jerry to admit his "super saint" behavior was his response to his dad's alcoholism. Ironically, his behavior was a normal way of coping with an abnormal situation. Like any child living with an alcoholic parent, he simply tried to survive.

Jerry's life revolved around trying to repair his broken, hurting family. He became the sole emotional support for both his mother and father. When Dad drank—which was nightly—Jerry would try to calm and console his irate mother. And he'd cover for his drunk dad in hopes of a peaceful night to do homework. Often Jerry put his dad to bed, only to be awakened in the wee hours by the metallic "pooosh!"

of a stashed, warm beer being opened.

When he saw his efforts had no effect, Jerry began even to feel responsible for the family's problem. He unconsciously began compensating for his family problems through public success. Public perfection became a way of life. By his senior year Jerry's achievements were astounding. His yearbook told the story: football team captain; student-senate president; newspaper editor; concert band member; basketball yell-leader; theater-production star.

Yet all Jerry's success never stopped Dad's drinking. It never brought peace at home. It didn't even disguise the family's problem from the town's intrusive stares. In truth, everything just got worse.

The worse his home life became, the harder Jerry worked. He was obsessed with perfection—publicly and personally. If something wasn't perfect, he'd try even harder to fix it. When he couldn't fix it, he'd turn his attention to polishing up the perfect. By making the strong stronger he compensated for the weak.

Or so he thought.

Breakdown

Jerry still isn't sure what happened. Unrelenting school pressures, a sports injury, girlfriend troubles and the ever-present stress at home wore him down. After months of working to keep it all together, Jerry collapsed—exhausted and convulsing in a frenzy of tears. Jerry remembers little that happened after he broke down. His only memory is a 120-day fog.

It was during that time, just before his 18th birthday, that Jerry first thought seriously of suicide. He'd always been able to handle anything through effort or denial. But now he was shaken. Out of control. Imperfect. Even worse, he didn't know what was wrong or why it had happened.

The breakdown haunted Jerry. What if it happened again? He convinced himself he must be going insane. And if that were the case, he thought, suicide would be a more honorable end for his life than an asylum.

Jerry worked out an acceptable suicide plan and decided to keep living as long as he could keep control. If he seemed about to break again, he'd just follow his plan. He couldn't bear going through that fog again. If Jerry hadn't received treatment as a young adult, he might have carried out his suicide plan.

Shared Story, Shared Pain

This book is about teenagers like Jerry. They're children of alcoholics (COAs). These young people aren't hard to find. They attend our youth groups each week. They come from every kind of home—even those that profess to be Christian.

According to the Children of Alcoholics Foundation, approximately 30 million Americans have at least one alcoholic parent. Thus one out of every eight people was raised or currently lives in an alcoholic family.[1] The average classroom of 25 will have four to six children of alcoholics. Sadly, only 5 percent of these children receive help.[2]

But while they're often all around us—in our youth groups and schools—they're not easy to spot. Their wounds are disguised behind fine-tuned survival responses. We dismiss some of these teenagers as hopelessly rebellious. We overlook others because they're ideal group members. Still others keep us laughing so hard at their outward antics that we don't see the crying inside. And some seem so private, so personal, that we're intimidated by their invisible walls.

If you're a youth worker with an average youth group of 20 to 25 kids, you probably have four to six youth group members who are children of alcoholics.[3]

Startling, isn't it?

Of course, the pain may be more or less evident in different teenagers. But regardless of how well these kids hide it, the suffering still festers behind the masks.

Kids at Risk

While these children of alcoholics may hide their pain behind perfection or humor or rebellion, their masks are made from papier-mâché that crumbles under pressure. These children desperately need the church's ministry. Growing up in an alcoholic family means facing both immediate risks and long-range consequences. These include:

Family violence—Alcohol contributes heavily to the number of child-abuse cases reported each year. Conservative estimates indicate that 55 percent of all family violence occurs in alcoholic homes.[4] The National Association for Children of Alcoholics (NACoA) sets this figure at 90 percent.[5] Clearly, well over one-half of the child-abuse cases involve alcohol abuse.

Incest—The daughter of an alcoholic father is twice as likely as her peers to be the victim of incest, according to the Do It Now Foundation.[6] In her book *It Will Never Happen to Me!* COA counselor Dr. Claudia Black claims that 26 percent of her clients have been incest victims. She contends that most incest occurs in these cases between alcoholic fathers or step-fathers and their daughters.[7]

In addition, Dr. Black asserts that many counselors who work with alcoholic women report that 60 to 80 percent of their clients have been incest victims.[8] Incest is so prevalent in alcoholic families that counselor and author Earnie Larsen assumes his female clients from alcoholic families have been sexually abused until therapy clearly reveals otherwise.[9]

Birth defects—Children born to alcoholic mothers are at high risk for Fetal Alcoholic Syndrome (FAS), now among the three leading causes of birth defects, according to the National Council on Alcoholism. (Down's syndrome and spina bifida are the other two.) FAS afflicts 1,800 to 2,400 infants each year. Another 36,000 infants are born with less-severe birth defects known as Fetal Alcohol Effects (FAE). Of the three leading causes of birth defects, FAS is the only preventable one.[10]

Frequent health problems—U.S. Department of

Health and Human Services researchers compared families in which alcoholism was not known to be present and families with at least one alcoholic member. They found that alcoholic families needed health care facilities more than nonalcoholic families. And the alcoholic families' medical costs were almost twice as high as other families.[11]

These statistics aren't surprising given the higher rate of stress-related disorders in alcoholic families: depression, anxiety, headaches, eating disorders, sleep disorders, ulcers, fatigue and colitis. Additionally, children of alcoholics tend toward learning difficulties, suicide and compulsive overachieving, according to the NACoA.[12]

Predisposition to addiction—The Do It Now Foundation claims that children of alcoholics are themselves three to four times as likely to become alcoholics as the general population.[13] Newsweek similarly reported that one out of four COAs become addicted to alcohol—compared to one out of 10 in the general population.[14]

If COAs don't become alcohol-dependent, they usually turn to something else. Seventy percent will indulge in compulsive behavior as an adult—gambling, overeating, smoking, excessive use of caffeine, compulsive exercising, excessive sleeping or spending, workaholism or drug abuse.[15]

Unhealthy relationships—A child from an alcoholic family is drawn to unhealthy relationships. Half of all children of alcoholics marry an alcoholic. And if a COA doesn't marry an alcoholic, he or she is likely to marry someone who also grew up in an alcoholic or otherwise troubled family.

Antisocial behavior—The National Association for Children of Alcoholics claims a disproportionate number of teenagers from alcoholic families enter the juvenile justice system, prisons, mental health institutions and courts.[16]

Each year I give a talk to pre-delinquent and delinquent teenagers at several denomination-sponsored group homes. The residents of the homes are most often sent there by the courts. On my last visit, I tested the NACoA's claim. I asked each group to indicate which kids came from homes in which at least one parent was an alcoholic. Never did the number of raised hands fall below half the total.

After reading this list of problems, you'd think it would be easy to identify COAs. It's not. Their problems frequently remain hidden because children of alcoholics learn survival techniques that our society accepts—even approves of. That's how Jerry could get through high school and into his adult career without detection.

A Peek Behind the Masks

People have only recently begun paying attention to children of alcoholics. Society's first concern was the alcoholic. Then we learned that spouses also suffered. But the focus remained on these two for many years. Finally, in the early '70s, we began noticing the traumatized children standing in the corner. Today a growing movement in chemical-dependency treatment is working to help children of alcoholics.

While the progress in the helping professions has been substantial, the church—with few exceptions—hasn't participated in this important ministry of healing. Too often the church has not recognized the problem or, worse, ignored it.

I once asked a COA friend whether her church had acknowledged her family's problem when she was a teenager. "It's really weird," she answered. "It did and yet it didn't. Each Christmas we'd receive a care package of food and gifts from the church. Dad had a job that should have adequately taken care of us. It's just that he drank his paychecks . . . Our poverty was obvious and must have hinted that something was wrong. But no one ever asked why we were poor. No one."

I hope this book will raise awareness among the people in the church who can best help: youth workers. Youth workers can reach out to these hurting teenagers and give them the hope and healing they need to avert the kind of crisis Jerry experienced.

This book gives youth workers the information needed to identify and respond to these hurting young people.

You'll have opportunities to evaluate your own ministry's effectiveness in reaching these young people. This book also provides practical tools for developing an effective ministry to these teenagers. If you're a child of an alcoholic yourself, you'll find information on how your family background affects your ministry and how to use your experience as a vehicle for ministry.

A ministry to teenagers from alcoholic families starts when we dare to look behind the hurt-hiding masks these young people wear. We need to ask questions that will help us discover the hidden problems. For only when we discover the problems can we begin to help.

But where do we start? We begin with awareness of the problem and its implications. That's the focus of the next three chapters. Part 2 then addresses a foundation and guidelines for this unique ministry.

Work It Out

1. What prompted you to read this book? List the concerns and questions you had when you started reading. Add questions this chapter raises about your ministry and youth group. Refer to your questions and concerns as you read the rest of the book.

2. Think about your "ideal youth group member." Does he or she resemble Jerry?

3. In the section titled Kids at Risk on page 20, highlight or underline clues for identifying COAs. Do these clues fit any kids in your youth group?

4. List five ways to "peek behind the mask" of a teenager like Jerry who appears successful, together, nearly perfect. How can you discover if everything is as good as it seems?

Endnotes

[1]Christina Parker, "Children of Alcoholics: Growing Up Unheard," (Phoenix, AZ: Do It Now Foundation, 1986).

[2]Vicky Lytle, "Children of Alcoholics: Recognizing Their 'Secret' Suffering," NEA Today (December 1987), 9.

[3]Eugene C. Roehlkepartain (editor), The Youth Ministry Resource Book (Loveland, CO: Group Books, 1988), 192; and Lytle, "Children of Alcoholics: Recognizing Their 'Secret' Suffering," 9.

[4]Parker, "Children of Alcoholics: Growing Up Unheard."

[5]Lytle, "Children of Alcoholics: Recognizing Their 'Secret' Suffering," 9.

[6]Parker, "Children of Alcoholics: Growing Up Unheard."

[7]Claudia Black, It Will Never Happen to Me! (Denver, CO: M.A.C. Communications, 1981), 141.

[8]Black, It Will Never Happen to Me!, 141.

[9]Earnie Larsen, "For Adult Children of Alcoholics and Those Who Love Them" (audio tape series) (Brooklyn Park, MN: E. Larsen Enterprises, 1984).

[10]"Facts on Alcohol-Related Birth Defects" (New York: The National Council on Alcoholism, 1987).

[11]"Treatment for Alcoholism—Impact on Use of Health Care," Uamha Update (July 1986).

[12]Lytle, "Children of Alcoholics: Recognizing Their 'Secret' Suffering," 9.

[13]Parker, "Children of Alcoholics: Growing Up Unheard."

[14]Charles Leerhsen, "Alcohol and the Family," Newsweek (January 18, 1988), 63.

[15]Parker, "Children of Alcoholics: Growing Up Unheard" and "Children of Alcoholics" (South Deerfield, MA: Channing L. Bete Co., 1986), 9.

[16]Cited in Lytle, "Children of Alcoholics: Recognizing Their 'Secret' Suffering," 9.

CHAPTER 2

Understanding Alcoholism

How Alcohol Affects the Alcoholic

Gretchen, a student, describes herself as an occasional, light drinker. She says she drinks only two or three times a year—and then only a couple of drinks.

To most people, that drinking pattern sounds innocent enough. Gretchen can't handle two drinks. She "blacks out," losing touch with where she is and what she's doing. She can't even be sure she stops after two drinks. As a result, she usually gets picked up by a guy at the dance or party. Later that night—maybe even the next morning—she wakes up and finds herself in the sack with a guy she doesn't know.

As a result of these episodes, Gretchen misses work, falls behind on school assignments and lies to her parents. And she carries a heavy load of guilt.

Is Gretchen an alcoholic?

People frequently make the mistake of identifying alcoholics by the outward signs alone: how much they drink, how often they drink, what they look like, how they behave in public. This mistaken idea feeds the myth that most alcoholics live on skid row. In fact, alcoholism often has nothing to do with the amount, frequency or other visible signs. Focusing on these traits only contributes to the myths about alcoholics. In reality, only 3 to 5 percent of alcoholics in the United States are on the streets. About 70 percent of alcoholics are married, working, everyday family people.[1]

The problem doesn't just concern inner-city rescue missions. It leaves its mark in cities, suburbs and rural communities. It affects the poor, the rich and the people in between. Altogether, an estimated 10 million adults and 3.3 million teenagers in the United States are alcoholics.[2]

Before you can minister effectively to families of alcoholics, you need to see beyond the myths about alcoholism. You need to develop an accurate picture of alcoholism and how it affects people's lives. Then you'll be better able to identify and minister to the children of alcoholics.

Identification of the Alcoholic

Since outward signs aren't usually adequate for identifying an alcoholic, what signs can you use? In the 1930s, Dr. Robert Seliger of Johns Hopkins University Hospital developed a questionnaire to help people determine whether they are alcoholics. Here's the questionnaire:

1. Do you lose time from work due to drinking? Yes ☐ No ☐

2. Is drinking making your home life unhappy? Yes ☐ No ☐

3. Do you drink because you are shy with other people? Yes ☐ No ☐

4. Is drinking affecting your reputation? Yes ☐ No ☐

5. Have you ever felt remorse after drinking? Yes ☐ No ☐

6. Have you gotten into financial difficulties as a result of drinking? Yes ☐ No ☐

7. Do you turn to lower companions and an inferior environment when drinking? Yes ☐ No ☐

8. Does your drinking make you careless
of your family's welfare?   Yes ☐   No ☐
9. Has your ambition decreased since
drinking?   Yes ☐   No ☐
10. Do you crave a drink at a definite time
daily?   Yes ☐   No ☐
11. Do you want a drink the next morning?   Yes ☐   No ☐
12. Does drinking cause you to have difficulty in sleeping?   Yes ☐   No ☐
13. Has your efficiency decreased since
drinking?   Yes ☐   No ☐
14. Is drinking jeopardizing your job or
business?   Yes ☐   No ☐
15. Do you drink to escape from worries or
trouble?   Yes ☐   No ☐
16. Do you drink alone?   Yes ☐   No ☐
17. Have you ever had a complete loss of
memory as a result of drinking?   Yes ☐   No ☐
18. Has your physician ever treated you for
drinking?   Yes ☐   No ☐
19. Do you drink to build up your self-
confidence?   Yes ☐   No ☐
20. Have you ever been to a hospital or institution on account of drinking?   Yes ☐   No ☐

A "yes" answer to just one question warns that the person might be an alcoholic. A "yes" answer to any two questions indicates probable alcoholism. And a "yes" answer to three or more questions clearly indicates alcoholism.

Another way to identify alcoholics is to look for these symptoms, which have been outlined by Dr. Terence McCormally, former medical director at the Riverview Rehabilitation Center in Iowa:

● Heavy drinking patterns that include drinking in the morning, hiding liquor, drinking to intoxication or trying to control drinking.

● Bizarre behavior that causes social, job, legal and family trouble, such as family violence, drunk driving or public intoxication.

● Physical addiction, which is often characterized by a high tolerance of alcohol and withdrawal symptoms in its absence.

Alcoholism's Effect on the Alcoholic

However you identify alcoholics, the problem is serious. The National Council on Alcoholism says alcoholics are people "whose drinking causes a continuing problem in any area of their lives."[3] It describes alcoholism as chronic, progressive and potentially fatal. Of course, alcoholism develops in different ways in different people. For some, it develops quickly. For others, it takes a lifetime.

Alcoholism takes a horrible toll on its victims. Most apparent are its physical effects:

● Each year about 95,000 people die from diseases caused by alcoholism or in alcohol-related accidents, homicides and suicides.[4]

● The connection between liver disease and alcoholism is indisputable and widely recognized.

● An alcoholic's appearance may change because of prolonged drinking. For example, W.C. Fields suffered from rhinophyma (a swollen, reddened "whiskey nose") and acne rosacea (a flushed, "spider web" appearance on the face caused by broken capillaries under the skin).

● Alcohol amblyopia—a disease that blurs a drinker's vision—is common among longtime drinkers.

● Heavy alcohol use affects the brain, nervous system, heart, stomach, pancreas and muscles. Alcoholism may also complicate diseases such as cancer and diabetes.

● Alcoholics are at higher risk for accidents. One study found that half of all people who die in falls have been drinking.[5] Alcoholics are 10 times as likely to die in fires as non-alcoholics.[6]

● Finally, the correlation between drunk driving and death is well-documented. Alcohol is involved in about half of all traffic fatalities. Each year, approximately 25,000 people die in alcohol-related car accidents.[7]

The Alcoholic as Addict

When I read the symptoms of alcoholism, I'm baffled that no one in my family saw how perfectly they fit my father. We knew he abused alcohol. But we didn't see him as an addict.

My family wasn't different from many alcoholic families in this regard. The line between abuse and addiction is sometimes so thin it seems invisible. Yet the two are different.

Strangely, some people can go on drinking binges and cause a few problems, yet remain free of dependency on alcohol. They are alcohol abusers but not addicts. If they were to complete the Johns Hopkins University Hospital questionnaire on page 26, these people would have one or two "yes" answers. But though they take significant risks with alcohol, they're not necessarily alcoholics.

The key difference between alcohol abuse and addiction is control. Does the user have control over the alcohol? Or does the alcohol have control over the user? Writing in *A Straight Word to Kids and Parents*, Dr. Anderson Spickard and Barbara Thompson help us understand the difference: "While the alcohol abuser chooses to get drunk, the alcoholic drinks involuntarily. Telling an alcohol addict to shape up and stop drinking is like telling a man who jumps out of a nine-story building to fall only three floors."[8]

One drug and alcohol counselor put it this way: An alcoholic is a person who "can't not drink." The grammar may be awkward, but the concept is sound. Alcoholics have little control over when they drink, how much they drink, what results from their drinking. Some depend so heavily on alcohol that they can't decide whether they'll drink. It's a given—if they have a chance, they'll drink. They no longer have a choice.

No other person wanted my dad to stop drinking more than he did. I can still remember times—sober and drunk— when he'd hug me and ask me to pray that he could stop drinking. Usually, because I was disgusted by what I saw as his weakness, I'd tell him to pray himself. With great sobs, he'd tell me he was too ashamed even to talk to God.

I have no doubt that Dad tried hard not to drink. Yet, he never overcame his alcoholism. Sure, he'd dry up for a few days, even weeks. But it never lasted. In the end he'd always come home smelling of beer. His eyes would be glazed, and he'd be sullen and silent.

Each time Dad tried to quit, the subsequent failure only intensified his feelings of shame and guilt. Ironically, these negative feelings added more reasons to drink again. Then it would take even more effort to stop drinking the next time. But he'd grow sick of his own drunkenness, and he'd try again. And the inevitable fall would be even harder. Thus the cycle went, year after year.

A Life-Consuming Problem

To understand the alcoholic family, we must see the alcoholic as an addict. While the "Just Say No" campaign means confidence for those who have already said no and hope for the abuser, it only means frustration, guilt and failure for the addict.

We quickly accept that the heroin, crack or cocaine addicts are dependent on their drugs. We know they cannot simply walk away from their addiction. But we expect the alcoholic just to walk away. We forget—or don't realize—the alcoholic's problem is more than a habit he or she can break at will. The alcoholic is *dependent* on alcohol. That's what it means to be an addict.

Thus alcoholism becomes a life-consuming problem for the addict. It affects not only the user, but also the user's family. That's the focus of the next chapter.

Work It Out

1. Imagine you're Gretchen. Answer the Johns Hopkins University Hospital questionnaire on page 26. In your opinion, is Gretchen an alcoholic? Explain your answer.

2. Read again the National Council on Alcoholism's description of an alcoholic (page 28). List several "continuing problems" that might indicate a person is an alcoholic.

3. How does your church define alcoholism and identify alcoholics? Compare and contrast that to the information in the section titled Identification of the Alcoholic on page 26.

4. How does the distinction between alcohol abuse and addiction affect your view of alcoholics? How might it affect your ministry?

Endnotes

[1]"Drinking Myths," (Topeka, KS: National Institute on Alcohol Abuse and Alcoholism, n.d.), 5.

[2]"1984 Facts on Alcoholism and Alcohol-Related Problems" (New York: National Council on Alcoholism, 1984); and Eugene C. Roehlkepartain (editor), *The Youth Ministry Resource Book*, (Loveland, CO: Group Books, 1988), 132.

[3]"1984 Facts on Alcoholism and Alcohol-Related Problems."

[4]"1984 Facts on Alcoholism and Alcohol-Related Problems."

[5]Robert O'Brien and Dr. Morris E. Chafetz (editors), *The Encyclopedia of Alcoholism* (New York: Facts on File, 1982), 2.

[6]O'Brien and Chafetz (editors), *The Encyclopedia of Alcoholism*, 3.

[7]"1984 Facts on Alcoholism and Alcohol-Related Problems."

[8]Dr. Anderson Spickard and Barbara Thompson, "A Sin—Or a Disease?" in *A Straight Word to Kids and Parents*, edited by the Hutterian Brethren (Rifton, NY: Plough Publishing House, 1987), 56.

CHAPTER 3

Living by "The Rules"

What Makes Alcoholic Families Different?

Grief-stricken by the stillbirth of what would have been her only daughter, Becky began to drink. A drink before bed relaxed her frantic mind and calmed her troubled heart. Having numbed her raging feelings, she slept in relative peace. That's Chris' memory of his mom.

> For as long as I can remember, I don't think
> my mom was sober for more than 10 days.

"The drink" wasn't consistent with the family's values about alcohol. But Becky's husband, Charles, stopped protesting when he saw how it seemed to help her. The raw emotion that flowed from Becky's pain was more than he could bear. He even began to look forward to the quiet that Becky's evening drink brought. Since "the drink" came after their bedtime, neither Chris nor his 5-year-old brother, Carl, could complain. Besides, they were too young to have a say in the matter.

Gradually "the drink" became two, then three, then

four, then innumerable. It also came earlier and earlier. Soon it didn't wait for the kids to go to bed. When Chris started school, "the drink" had invaded dinner. When he was in fourth grade, he and Carl would return from school to find Mom alone with "the drink."

At first Becky managed to maintain a strong job performance. "Performance" accurately describes her behavior. She worked hard to conceal the alcohol's effects. Other social workers had been fired for drinking, so she knew she was taking a risk.

For a time, Becky also maintained a strong front at church. She and Charles regularly attended Sunday school and worship. Their faith had always been central to their lives. Chris and Carl had been taken to church activities weekly from birth.

But Becky couldn't hide the change at home. Family life changed dramatically. "The drink" became the focus of Becky's life. Chris' childhood mental picture of his mother shows her glass clasped in her left hand. It went everywhere with her. Family members became so accustomed to seeing her with the glass of booze that they unconsciously brought it to her on rare occasions when she walked off without it. It even had a name: Mom's Glass. No one—repeat, no one—but her ever drank from it.

As "the drink" became part of the family, Becky gradually left the family. Charles began using his lunch hour to do household chores. While Becky sometimes missed work because of hangovers, Charles sometimes missed work to care for their home and the boys. Both grew concerned that their performance reviews would reflect their frequent absences.

Then the fights started. Chris remembers the first one. He was 7.

> Mom had been drinking and was pretty well
> out of it. Dad was telling her enough was enough
> and that he couldn't cover for her anymore. He
> took the glass out of her hand and shattered it on

the floor.

Mom screamed, jumped out of her chair, and started to swing at Dad. He backed away at first. Then he jumped at her and pushed her backward over her chair. Dad walked into the living room, sat down and started to bawl. Mom lay crying on the floor.

Things were never the same between them again. It's strange, but as obvious as it was, we didn't admit there was even a fight. But then we never talked about the drinking either.

The fights continued. They didn't always involve physical violence, but Chris clearly remembers the verbal violence. As the emotional distance grew between Charles and Becky, stronger emotional bonds developed between the parents and the boys. Charles and Carl grew closer, and Chris latched on to Becky. Chris liked his special relationship with his mom, but he later realized it was unhealthy.

I took the place of my dad emotionally and psychologically. Mom would talk to me—tell me things a 10-year-old ought not hear from his mom. Things like how she felt about Dad, her excuses for drinking, and how bad she hurt because my sister had died. I listened, I hugged her, and I wiped her tears when she cried. But it never felt right.

By the time Chris was 12, Charles and Becky were so far apart that they might as well not have been married. Just before his 13th birthday, Chris' family split up. One night Charles didn't come home. He just called to say he was staying with a friend and was filing for divorce.

The divorce wasn't as bad as Chris had feared. His parents wanted to maintain an air of respectability about the family, and they didn't want Becky's drinking to become public. Chris and Carl were given a choice of where they wanted to live. Carl chose Dad. Chris stayed with Mom.

> I felt like I had to stay with her. I mean,
> there was no one left to look after her. I'd think
> about ways she could hurt herself when she
> drank. I even worried about things—like how
> she'd make it to work in the morning without
> someone to help her. Who'd be there for her
> when she felt sad? I couldn't live with the guilt
> of leaving her.
> I didn't want to go home with her either—I
> knew I would be in for a lot of work. But in the
> end, my guilt won.

Chris was right. It *was* a lot of work. And he hadn't expected some of the hardship. For example, the family had
basically been able to afford what it needed. The double income hid the reality of how much his mother spent on
booze. With just one paycheck, each dollar became important. But if Chris' mom had her way, everything she earned
would pay for "the drink."

Chris usually snatched his mom's paycheck after she en-
dorsed it to be sure they had money for bills, groceries and
his own spending money. But sometimes he wasn't clever or
fast enough. Those were lean weeks.

Despite the difficulties, Chris recognized some advan-
tages. He soon learned how to get anything he wanted from
his mom, either by asking at the right time in the drinking
cycle or by playing on his mom's guilt.

Chris also set his own schedule. If he cared for his
mother first by making dinner and cleaning the house, Chris
could do whatever he wanted with his time. He found his
niche in the church. He continued to attend faithfully, eventually joining the church and becoming youth group president.

Alcohol's Effect on the Family

As Chris' story illustrates, alcohol not only affects the alcoholic, but it shapes the whole family. In the book *Broken Bottles, Broken Dreams: Understanding and Helping the Children of Alcoholics*, author Charles Deutsch identifies five overarching conditions that exist in alcoholic families, in varying degrees:

- Focus on the alcoholic and alcohol-related behavior;
- Denial and shame;
- Inconsistency, insecurity and fear;
- Anger and hatred; and
- Guilt and blame.[1]

These conditions don't just result from overt negative behavior such as abuse and violence. They also grow out of covert negative behavior such as the lack of affirmation, communication or interaction. In an article in the Recovery Life insert of Alcoholism and Addiction journal, COA therapist Dr. Claudia Black notes that trauma in these families results more from "what does *not* occur than by what *does* occur."[2] She suggests three questions to help family members assess the covert negative behaviors in their families:

- What didn't you *hear* from your parent (such as words of affirmation and love)?
- What didn't you get to *say* to that parent (such as talk about school problems, tell about friendship)?
- What didn't you get to *do* with that parent (such as go to the park or ball games, play games together)?[3]

These questions point to some of the pain in alcoholic families. But while the family suffers from the alcoholism, ironically it also can perpetuate it. Alcoholism doesn't exist in a void. The alcoholic "needs" other family members to create and maintain an environment where the addiction thrives. Thus alcoholic homes are sick, crazy places to live.

Bill's dad started drinking to relieve job stress. Within months he'd lost control. This only added stress, because he feared being discovered. So to keep up at the office, he brought more and more work home with him. But his drinking kept him from doing any of it. To be helpful, Bill's mother did some of the work for him—occasionally working all night long. And Bill's dad still drank.

Charly's mom was a minister. And an alcoholic. Her mom told the whole family never to tell anyone that she occasionally took a drink. "They wouldn't understand," she said. No one ever told. Not even on that Easter morning when the whole family stepped in to lead the worship service because the pastor had "taken ill" the night before.

On three occasions Jill and her mother packed up and left during her dad's drunks. Each time they vowed to never go back. But as they ran out of money, they started worrying. So, believing it better to live with a drunk who could support them than to live on the streets, they returned.

Different Rules

To understand the dynamics of these families, we must realize that they operate with a different set of "rules" from healthy families. These rules, which evolve over time in response to alcoholic behavior, shape the family and its members. Alcoholism knocks the whole family out of balance, and family members struggle just to survive.

While I was receiving treatment as a child of an alcoholic, I saw a film titled *The Family Trap*. In it, noted COA therapist and author Sharon Wegscheider-Cruse compares the family to a mobile. A mobile is a beautiful art form because of its delicate balance and graceful movement. Though constructed only of string and sticks, it has uncommon strength and resilience. When you exert pressure on any part of a mobile, the whole structure shifts, changes and even swings about. But it always maintains its balance, returning finally to the equilibrium it enjoyed before the tension.

In the healthy family, pressures sometimes force shifts and changes but the family maintains its balance and eventually returns to normal equilibrium. In contrast, the alcoholic family is like a mobile in which one of the weights has been damaged or even removed. The whole mobile must then find a new balance to compensate for the loss.

Though alcoholic and other dysfunctional families eventually find a new balance, the whole system is weaker. It's less able to absorb the pressures that typically confront all families.

This new balance also creates new family rules. A key to working with kids from alcoholic families is knowing how these rules work. In *It Will Never Happen to Me!* Dr. Claudia Black identifies and explains three primary rules: "don't talk," "don't trust" and "don't feel."[4]

"Don't Talk"—For a lot of reasons, Chris never talked about his mom's drinking:

● She'd been drinking since he could remember. It was normal to him.

● He and Carl had been told to never say anything to anyone about "the drink." Talking might jeopardize Becky's job or the family's reputation.

● If he talked he'd feel guilty for betraying the family.

● He wasn't sure anyone would even believe him.

● Nobody in his family talked about the problem—at least not in any sane, rational way.

Besides, even people who should have known something was wrong never asked about it. Chris remembers going to school with frequent stomachaches. He'd endure them as long as he could before asking to see the nurse. Each time he went, he'd get Pepto-Bismol and lie down until the cramps left. When tensions were really bad at home, he'd go through this routine three or four times a week. But despite his regular visits, the school nurse never asked any questions that might have given Chris a chance to tell the family secret.

The alcoholic family's code of silence is almost unbreakable. Comedian Louie Anderson illustrates how well he obeyed the "don't talk" rule in his alcoholic family. He tells about riding in a car with his drunk father late at night, when his dad lost control and crashed. Fortunately, no one was hurt. When neighbors arrived and offered to help, young Louie—answering for his passed-out dad and frightened little brother—simply answered "No."

"You see, my dad's drinking was a problem we weren't going to share with anyone," he later explained. "There was something wrong with my family, I realized, but it was private."[5]

No one can be an addict without a cover-up. Ann Wilson Schaef, writing in *Co-dependence: Misunderstood-Mistreated*, says, "An addiction is anything we feel we have to lie about."[6] The "don't talk" rule is the family's way of lying about the alcoholic's addiction, thus helping him or her maintain it. Though family members believe keeping the secret helps, it actually hurts the family by prolonging the cover-up and the arrival of real help.

This first rule and the dishonesty that surrounds it contribute to the second rule.

"Don't Trust"—Several years ago I heard a joke that I tell often, though it's not really funny:

Question: "How can you tell an alcoholic is lying?"

Answer: "His lips move."

Filled with self-hatred, fear and guilt, alcoholics resort to lying to rationalize their drinking. This dishonesty becomes a facade that says "everything's okay."

Where dishonesty rules, inconsistency runs rampant. When inconsistency runs rampant, life becomes unpredictable. And when life becomes unpredictable, trust eventually fades from the heart of a child.

God intends parents to protect, nurture, provide for and love their kids. Children of alcoholics quickly learn that alcoholism makes it difficult, even impossible, for their parent to fulfill these responsibilities.

When Mom and Dad are absorbed in "the problem," meals aren't fixed, clothes aren't washed, the house isn't cleaned, wages are lost and household bills go unpaid. Parents don't remember the promises they made to attend school or church events. And they're not emotionally available to comfort and assure their children. They may not even be home.

At these times, who do these children turn to? Who do they trust?

Chris answered this question like most COAs answer it: If no one seems trustworthy, trust only yourself. Through years of broken promises and disappointments, Chris learned that chaos was the only predictable thing about his family. The only person he was sure he could trust was himself.

When the "don't trust" rule operates in a family, each member builds a high, fortified wall of mistrust around himself or herself. Within the wall the person feels strangely invincible. All the faith that could have been placed in others is now focused on self.

Add the third rule of alcoholic families, and the COA's fortress is complete.

"Don't Feel"—This is the most harmful rule. Alcoholic families are in a lot of pain but don't have any way to deal with it. They could choose to feel it and express it, but because of the other two rules—"don't talk" and "don't trust"—COAs are afraid their feelings won't be accepted or supported. So they most often choose other ways to handle their pain.

First, they handle it by not handling it. Dr. Timmen Cermak, a co-founder of the National Association for Children of Alcoholics, calls this process "psychic numbing."[7] Others call it emotional repression or frozen feelings. Al-Anon, Adult Children of Alcoholics, and Alcoholics Anonymous groups call it "stuffing."

Whatever you call it, it's the "don't feel" rule in force.

Children of alcoholics frequently compare their home life to "walking on eggshells." They have to act in the most careful, unoffensive ways possible so they don't cause additional stress that could upset the family's fragile balance.

The "don't feel" rule is a way to manage the pain. Some children of alcoholics follow this rule so faithfully they can speak of unspeakable trauma without showing the slightest emotion.

A teenage COA once told me about her father sexually

abusing her. She was so young and small, she explained, he could not penetrate her at first. So he used a dull letter opener to enlarge the vaginal opening.

As she related this story, I could feel my own face redden and contort with anger and pain. Yet she didn't flinch. Her voice didn't change. Her face didn't flush. And her body language didn't betray discomfort. Nothing in her manner or speech even suggested anything bad had happened.

The Irony of the Rules

These family rules are primary ways kids learn to cope. But, ironically, the rules also make it even more difficult to cope.

The rules create a safe environment for the alcoholic to drink. They shut down all honest communication between family members. No one knows what others are doing. So the problem can remain unnamed and unchecked.

To illustrate, think of being at a party. The effervescent but gracious hostess has bad breath. All the guests know the problem, but no one mentions it. So what do they do? They avoid conversations with her. Talk stays on a superficial level to avoid extended contact. Thus the hostess avoids the problem and embarrassment. And the guests avoid the awkwardness of telling a difficult truth. Sadly, the hostess can't deal with the problem because no one is honest with her.

Avoiding the problem perpetuates the alcoholism. And denial prevents non-alcoholic members of the family from supporting one another. After all, if you won't confront the alcoholic about the problem, you're not going to talk about it with each other.

Now the irony: Though the family rules certainly contribute to the problem, they also help family members cope. Because they protect themselves by not trusting, feeling or talking, the children of alcoholics survive.

Life by the Rules

These three rules govern all areas of the COA's life. They dictate how children view and respond to their world. They regulate relationships. They follow the families everywhere—to school, to work, to church. They're always present in everything COAs do.

As a result, children of alcoholics will relate to you—the youth worker—and the youth group the same way they relate to their alcoholic family members. It's unrealistic to think otherwise, since those patterns are the only patterns they know. Of course, they can learn healthier ways to relate. But it won't happen overnight.

Each time I explain these rules to groups, someone always asks: "You know, I didn't grow up in an alcoholic family. In fact, my family was basically healthy. But I still remember times when these rules operated in our family. If they're rules of a sick family, why did we sometimes live by them?"

If I feel contentious I might answer, "Maybe your family wasn't as healthy as you think!" But that's not usually fair, and the good question deserves a good answer. Let's look at a couple of explanations.

Rules are normal. All families occasionally function under the "don't talk," "don't trust" and "don't feel" rules. They have little secrets that need to be kept. So you "don't talk." Sometimes family conflict shakes confidence, so you "don't trust" for a while. And even healthy families can sometimes be painful places, so you find emotional insulation in the "don't feel" rule.

These are normal reactions to the pressures any families feel. But in healthy families, these rules are temporary exceptions, not the day-to-day norm. If, for example, a family member dies, children in a healthy family may become numb to their emotional pain in order to cope. However, as the tragedy becomes a memory and the grief process takes its course, the children become more open and honest with their feelings.

Alcoholic families are different. They habitually and rigidly follow the rules all the time. The rules are automatic, unconscious responses to anything—good or bad—that disturbs the family.

Other families are also unhealthy. These rules aren't exclusive to alcoholic families. They flourish in other dysfunctional families. In his book *Lost in the Shuffle: The Codependent Reality*, Robert Subby identifies four family types that produce these rules:

● The alcoholic and chemically dependent family.

● The emotionally and/or psychologically disturbed family. The rules provide constancy and predictability when a family member behaves in unpredictable, inconsistent ways.

● The abusive family in which family members constantly fear being hurt physically, sexually or emotionally. The rules give a sense of security.

● The fundamentalist or rigidly religious family that tries to control family members' behavior by stressing discipline, order and compliance. These strict families enforce "the letter of the law" without grace. These families reinterpret the rules and identify them as virtuous and healthy.[8]

Healthy families provide love and affection for all members. They validate individuals' feelings, and each person receives nurturing. Yet even the healthiest families exist on a delicate balance between functional and dysfunctional, well and troubled.

In contrast, unless they receive outside help, alcoholic families stay trapped in the destructive rules. Thus family members integrate these rules into their personalities and lives. They learn to live with the crazy restrictions. The alcoholic finds peace in a bottle. The kids and spouse must find their own ways of coping. The next chapter shows how family members learn to cope and how these patterns affect them in future years.

While I want to stir you to concern and action, I don't want to paint an unfair portrait of these families. Like other parents, these parents want to give their children a loving, nurturing, caring, safe, stable environment. But a single force in the family siphons a disproportionate amount of time, energy and attention from the parents and their pursuit of these goals. Its name: alcoholism.

Speaking as I have about the alcoholic family isn't intended to label its members as evil or bad. They are frequently good, well-intentioned people. However, the alcoholic and spouse become obsessed with the addiction, and the children are left alone to get by the best they can.

Work It Out

1. How do you relate to Chris' story? How does it seem foreign to you? Do you know people who you suspect grew up in an environment like Chris'?

2. Look again at Chris' story. Think of people in Chris' life who could have helped Chris if they had known about the problem. What clues could have identified trouble at home?

3. From the list of conditions that Charles Deutsch identifies in alcoholic homes (page 37), which do you think are most damaging? How have you seen those conditions damage your own family or families you've known about?

4. What was your immediate reaction when you read the alcoholic family rules—"don't talk," "don't trust," "don't feel"? If you felt these rules in your own family, were they temporary or ongoing?

5. Brainstorm 10 things you could do in your youth group to counteract some youth group members' negative survival rules.

Endnotes

[1]Charles Deutsch, *Broken Bottles, Broken Dreams: Understanding and Helping the Children of Alcoholics*, (New York: Teachers College Press, 1982), 31.

[2]Claudia Black, "How Different is Recovery for a COA?" Alcoholism and Addiction (August 1988), in Recovery Life.

[3]Black, "How Different is Recovery for a COA?"

[4]Black, *It Will Never Happen to Me!* (Denver, CO: M.A.C. Communications, 1981), 33-46.

[5]Daniel Chu and Bonnie Johnson, "Breaking the Bond of Silence," People Weekly (April 18, 1988), 106.

[6]Ann Wilson Schaef, *Co-dependence: Misunderstood-Mistreated* (Minneapolis: Winston Press, 1986), 21.

[7]"Dr. Timmen Cermak, Who Has Been There, Shows the Way Out," People Weekly (April 18, 1988), 110.

[8]Robert Subby, *Lost in the Shuffle: The Co-dependent Reality* (Pompano Beach, FL: Health Communications, 1987), 10-11.

Behind the Masks

When Survival Becomes a Lifestyle

On her 14th birthday, Cindy made a special four-year calendar. On the very last date, her 18th birthday, she wrote, "I'm free!" Each night she took the calendar from its hiding place under her mattress and marked a large X over the date.

She was one day closer to her goal.

● ● ●

Phil had run away from home three times. The authorities had found him each time, and he returned. And each time the reprimand from both his parents and the authorities was stronger than the previous one. The last time it happened, he was grounded. Though the restriction ended only two weeks ago, Phil was planning a fourth attempt to escape.

● ● ●

Shari had planned the next six years of her life. She figured she could complete her master's degree in business by then. Since only three months separated high school graduation from the beginning of college, she thought she could stay busy enough to make it through the summer.

● ● ●

During his junior year of high school, Larry had arranged to join the Marine Corps. After selecting a job from
the list of options, he worked out a timetable with the
recruiter. To his relief, Larry would be inducted within a
week of his high school graduation.

● ● ●

If you met Cindy, Phil, Shari and Larry, you'd think they
had nothing in common. They live in the same Midwest
town, but they live at different social and economic levels.
Each has different friends and interests. And none would select one of the other three as a friend.

Still they're more alike than any would admit. Each lives
with an alcoholic parent. And each has found a way to survive in a "war zone."

The War Zone

Many of the young people who come into your church
from alcoholic families will already hold what Newsweek
calls the "M.D." degree—Masters of Disaster.[1] They understand what it takes to survive in a destructive, alcoholic
family.

Therapist Dr. Claudia Black identifies survival as a uni-
versal goal for children of alcoholics. She discovered that
each COA she counseled had pledged, "It will never happen
to me!" So common was this conviction among her clients
that it became the title of her ground-breaking book.[2]

Those who survive, so the story goes, are the ones
who . . .

● make it to adulthood alive . . .
● without becoming alcoholic and . . .
● establish a family that's healthier than the one they
left behind.

These may sound like reasonable goals to the outsider.
But they're major tasks for children of alcoholics.

People who have never lived in an alcoholic family may
question using the word "survival" to describe teenagers'

actions. It's an awfully strong word, isn't it? After all, they wonder, what could be "that bad"?

Yet many COAs can relate to images of the alcoholic family as a "war zone" and kids as "survivors." I once saw a TV interview with a Vietnam veteran who was also a child of an alcoholic. He said, "I consider growing up in an alcoholic home more traumatic than being in Vietnam."

I don't want to spark a debate between Vietnam vets and COAs about who has been more deeply wounded by their experiences. Only God knows the depth of hurt each carries. The man's statement simply underscores how ugly it can be to grow up in an alcoholic family.

Survival Roles

How do children learn to survive in this environment? In Chapter 3 we addressed one way: the family rules. There's also another way: Children in alcoholic families assume different roles. They naturally seek—even unknowingly—a way to get by until they can get out. (The alcoholic's spouse also takes a specific co-dependent role in the family. See "Understanding Co-Dependence" on page 50 for more information.)

Like the family rules, these roles mask the truth about the family's problems and the child's feelings. They're deceptive masks children of alcoholics wear to survive.

Just as the family doesn't consciously write its rules, neither does the child knowingly adopt a role. "Children growing up in alcoholic homes seldom learn the combinations of roles which mold healthy personalities," Dr. Black explains in *It Will Never Happen to Me!* "Instead, they become locked into roles based on their perception of what they need to do to 'survive' and to bring some stability to their lives."[3]

Because of the masks, teenagers with alcoholic parents come to our churches and youth groups incognito. They want, above all else, to appear normal. Often their disguises are ingenious. We're fooled into believing exactly what they

Understanding Co-Dependence

Co-dependence is a relatively new term that eludes any single concise definition. Yet you need to become familiar with the term if you want to minister to alcoholic families.

The non-drinking spouse becomes so caught up in the other's problem that he or she even begins to act like the alcoholic. Like the alcoholic, the spouse becomes unpredictable, moody, inconsistent and dishonest. He or she is as addicted to the alcoholic as the alcoholic is to the substance. But unlike the alcoholic, the spouse doesn't have intoxication as an excuse. So, to the kids, their non-drinking parent's behavior may seem crazier than that of the drinking parent.

That's why Chris (Chapter 3) had a hard time relating to his dad. Sure, his mom had the drinking problem, but at least she had a reason for the bizarre things she did. What else would you expect from a drunk? Chris expected something else from his dad.

As he grew up, Chris began to resent his father. By the time he reached adolescence, Chris even blamed his dad for his mom's drinking. Who wouldn't drink if she were married to such a nagging and critical husband?

Identification with the alcoholic is common when kids see the non-alcoholic parent abuse and harangue the drinker. Kids may also identify with the alcoholic when the non-drinking parent fails to rescue the children from the problem. The kids look to the non-drinking parent as their only hope; when he or she can't stop the other parent from drinking, the kids become disillusioned.

Kids can judge their non-drinking, co-dependent parents harshly. But if they could look inside their parents, they might be surprised by what they'd see:

● Low self-esteem that's bolstered only by others' approval
● Unrealistic expectations of perfection
● Difficulty identifying and expressing feelings
● Fear of conflict
● A sense of guilt from feeling overly responsible for the alcoholic's drinking—yet an inability to change it

want us to believe—all is well.

Sharon Wegscheider-Cruse has identified four roles teenagers from alcoholic families commonly assume:

- The Family Hero
- The Lost Child
- The Mascot
- The Scapegoat[4]

Imagine what it would be like if your youth group consisted of only four kids and each played one of these roles. Then suppose a crisis occurred in your imaginary group. For example, it was your turn to bring refreshments, but you forgot. How would these teenagers react if they acted strictly within their roles?

The Scapegoat would become so ticked that he'd call you a name and take a swing at you. To ease the tension the Mascot would joke about your absent-mindedness, then tease the Scapegoat for his failed punch. The Family Hero would jump up to protect you, shush the Mascot and offer to go buy some Oreos. And the Lost Child would move nearer the Family Hero and softly say, "Really, I'm not hungry anyway."

This imaginary illustration is ludicrous because of its extremes, but it helps us understand the different roles and how they interrelate in the family. When they act these ways, children of alcoholics can frighten, impress or entertain us. When we don't understand their motivation, they can strike us as being both funny "ha-ha" and funny "weird."

In the following pages we'll briefly look at how each of these roles might be played in your youth group. We'll elaborate on the characteristics outlined by Charles Deutsch in *Broken Bottles, Broken Dreams: Understanding and Helping the Children of Alcoholics*.[5] Keep in mind that you may see elements of several roles in a child of an alcoholic. However, one role frequently dominates.

The Family Hero

Do you need a teenager to plan, organize and lead your

annual youth service? What about that special event next month? Do you need someone to promote it by calling every group member? Are you looking for someone to clean up after a group party next week? Who're you gonna call? The Family Hero!

Heroes are rarely intimidated by the impossible. They love challenges. What kid can give 10 hours each week to the youth group, play a varsity sport, carry the lead in the spring musical, maintain a 4.0 grade-point average, edit the school newspaper, and still have a 30-minute personal devotional time each morning?

Yes, the Family Hero.

Family Heroes' superhuman behaviors make sense when you consider their role in the alcoholic family:

Care for the family—Family Heroes take care of everyone else, including their parents. They don't usually want the role at first; they receive it by default. Because both Mom and Dad are obsessed with the alcoholism, neither is available to be a parent. But someone needs to. So enter the Family Hero.

Respect and honor—Family Heroes bring the alcoholic family respect and honor. These superachieving kids receive frequent recognition from their schools, communities and churches. The Heroes crave this approval because it's their only source of self-esteem. It also proves—in their minds—that their family is normal.

The family craves approval and recognition for the Hero too. If the family catches a glimpse of its problem, it points to the Hero's personal success as proof of the family's success. Because they must fulfill their families' vicarious needs, Family Heroes carry tremendous burdens.

As we look at the outward Hero, we may think he or she has everything together. Yet hidden behind the mask is a wounded young person who wears the mask like a bandage to keep from reopening the wounds. Wegscheider-Cruse says that Heroes hide feelings of pain, inadequacy, confusion, guilt, fear and low self-esteem.[6]

Jerry, who you met in Chapter 1, is a Family Hero. Kids

like Jerry come close to fitting all your daydreaming about the ideal youth group member. Sometimes we use them as models for the rest of our group. They're excellent leaders. They take assignments seriously, attend regularly and are incredibly reliable. When Heroes say "yes" to something, you needn't worry whether it will get done. It will—ahead of schedule.

On those rare occasions they don't get everything done, they fall apart. They apologize profusely and explain their failure in detail—even when no explanation is needed.

Not only do Family Heroes take their youth group commitment seriously, they also take their faith seriously. However your church defines the faith journey, Family Heroes will be doggedly marching down the path. Family Heroes try to walk with Christ as perfectly as possible. Ironically, they usually don't come across like Pharisees. And no matter how hard they try, they never feel as if they've done well enough.

This drive to perfection can drive youth workers crazy. Sometimes you want to shake them and say: "Look, I'm glad you love God and want to serve him. But lighten up a little!"

One of the effects of taking themselves so seriously is that Heroes have few close friends. They have trouble just having fun. Besides, they're not trusting, vulnerable people. Instead, they need to be independent and in control— characteristics that don't promote good friendships. The friends they do make tend to be weak loser-types who need someone to take care of them. And the Hero gladly meets their needs.

Understanding the Family Hero's needs—Though Family Heroes are devoted to meeting the needs of others, they are themselves needy. They need to feel worthwhile.

Sadly, Heroes try to feel better about themselves by seeking compliments and praise. As youth workers, we can easily feed this craving for approval by focusing our praise on what they do, rather than who they are. In the process we miss their real need.

Family Heroes need *affirmation*, not *approval*. Approval focuses on the Hero's performance; affirmation focuses on the Hero as a person. We can help meet the Hero's need for affirmation by verbally and non-verbally communicating: "You always were, always are and always will be good enough. You have nothing to prove. Just be yourself as God created you—a unique, wonderful person. You can't impress me by what you do, because I'm already impressed with you as a person. I love you."

The Lost Child

Who's that youth group member whose name you can never quite remember? Stan? Or Steve? Maybe Sam? What *is* his name?

Just call him the Lost Child.

The Lost Children of alcoholic families are best known for not being known. They survive by avoiding conflict. They seek and take the path of least resistance, trying not to create problems or draw attention to themselves.

Don't expect Lost Children to participate in lively discussions—at least not willingly. Instead, look for them to sit at the edge of the group—as far to the edge as possible without actually being outside the group. They rarely take strong positions. If your group votes on activities, expect the Lost Child to respond: "I don't care. It really doesn't matter to me. Whatever we do will be just fine. I'm flexible."

Why do these kids adopt these roles? Let's look at some reasons:

Keeping the peace—I believe Lost Children most often attend youth group meetings when doing so keeps peace at home. The question is not whether they want to be at youth group. Rather, the question is: Where will I feel least threatened tonight? At youth group? At home? Or on a walk by myself? Most of the time they'd prefer a solitary walk. But they'll go to youth group if it's expected.

Minimizing risk—You'll be tempted to peg Lost Children as stupid or spacey or maybe even mentally impaired.

Don't be deceived. They're usually bright kids—maybe the most intelligent of all. They may pretend to not hear you, or to misunderstand instructions or even act as if they've forgotten what you expected of them. But they do this because they've learned that appearing ignorant is the best way to minimize risk. Also, people just leave them alone. And with no contact, there's no risk of conflict.

Not attracting attention—What do these kids give their families? Relief. No one has to worry about the Lost Child. Out of trouble. Out of sight. Out of mind. The family can concentrate on other things.

But while these children don't cause problems, they hide them. They feel unimportant, lonely and abandoned. They've been defeated by the problem, and they're unwilling to risk doing anything to help themselves.

Understanding the Lost Child's needs—While Lost Children seek to be *anonymous* in your group, they need to become *autonomous*. For the sake of safety and security, Lost Children have forfeited their capacity to operate independently.

We can help the Lost Child by helping him or her discover autonomy. This begins by developing a trusting friendship with the Lost Child. It won't be easy, since the Lost Child survives by remaining distant. We must nurture our relationship patiently yet firmly, paying close attention to the signals the Lost Child sends. When the signal is to back off, we do. When the signal is to move ahead, we do so carefully.

Once we've established our friendship, we can begin to encourage the Lost Child to take some appropriate risks in relationships—risks that will probably succeed. For example, we could encourage a Lost Child to talk with a teacher about a grade that seems unfair. This experience would encourage the Lost Child to think independently, face conflict, express feelings and take a stand. Enough of these successful experiences will nurture the teenager's sense of autonomy.

Throughout this friendship process, it's critical that we respect the Lost Child's personal boundaries. We can't make him or her come out of the shell. Indeed, if we use force, we simply reinforce a well-known pattern: To keep peace, give in to others.

The Mascot

Imagine a 16-year-old with the zaniness of Jonathan Winters, the machine-gun delivery of Robin Williams, the aggressiveness of Don Rickles and the comedic timing of Steve Martin. Got that image fixed in your mind? That's your Mascot!

If you'd like more Family Heroes in your group, you'll wish you didn't have any Mascots. Mascots are the kids you love and hate. You love their sense of humor and spontaneity. But you hate it when they use it on you. They're the kids you are most likely to call "jerk," "turkey" and other less loving names under your breath.

While these kids are difficult to have in a group, they serve important roles in their alcoholic families:

Easing tension—Mascots are the alcoholic family's court jester. A jester's role was to keep the king merry, particularly in times of stress and tension. Sometimes called "fools," jesters were actually brilliant. They knew all the latest news, and they created hilarious jokes out of current events and even sensitive issues. Jesters knew just when their humor was needed and how far to push it.

Masking the pain—Mascots use humor to relax the family in the midst of nearly constant tension. If they can keep the family laughing, they reason, things can't be all that bad. It's a way of masking their own pain.

In social settings such as youth group activities, Mascots respond to tension the same way they respond to it at home. That's great fun at a party or if the group is doing something crazy. But it's obtrusive and distressing during reflection and worship times. When Mascots feel insecure or threatened, they'll do something cute or humorous to break the tension.

That's why you hope they won't be at the next Bible

study or youth group worship. You pray: "Please, God, nothing serious. Just a cold that's bad enough to keep them home." But they show up. They always do, because they need an audience.

I once led a group with a non-stop talking Mascot. Throughout the meeting he maintained a running commentary with his neighbor. This Mascot didn't need the whole group to laugh as long as one person did. His accomplice was all too willing to play along.

Everyone enjoys having Mascots around—for awhile. But Mascots just don't shut off. Their self-esteem is tied to keeping people laughing. So they keep coming at you. It becomes unbearable, and you walk away. The Mascots are left alone—feeling abandoned, lonely and inadequate. "What's wrong with me?" they ask themselves. "Maybe I wasn't funny enough. Well, there's always next time . . ."

Understanding the Mascot's needs—To help Mascots, we need to understand their need for assurance. But in the process of seeking *assurance*, Mascots settle for *automation*—operating in a predictable, familiar way that may be ultimately harmful, but at least it seems safe for now.

We help Mascots when we convey to them that stress and conflict are normal parts of family life. All families have both. The difference is that healthy families face stress and conflict instead of running away from them or denying them.

Mascots also must learn that everything doesn't need to be funny. Emotional responses besides laughter are okay and appropriate. Mascots need to see it's okay to feel even the most negative emotions for a time. If we can assure Mascots that the absence of laughter isn't a sign of impending disaster, we've taken an important step toward helping them.

The Scapegoat

You probably won't have many Scapegoats in your youth group. They're not exactly into doing socially accepted things like going to church. When Scapegoats do attend,

one of several things is probably true:
- Someone told them not to come.
- They're looking for trouble.
- They've found trouble you haven't discovered yet.
- Your meetings speak to a deep, vulnerable need in them.

In some ways, Scapegoats are the most honest with their feelings. They act out what the Family Heroes, Lost Children, and Mascots feel but can't express. Scapegoats just express feelings in inappropriate ways.

They're called Scapegoats because—like the scapegoat of the Old Testament who bore the sins of the Hebrews—they bear their families' "sins." They divert attention from the real, secret problem. And they're often blamed for the real problem: "Your mom drinks because she's worried about you always being in trouble." They may also be used as an excuse for the alcoholic behavior: "You'd drink too if you had a daughter who worried you as much as she worries me."

When Scapegoats do come to our youth groups, our first reaction is to judge them the same way their families do. Their outward appearances reinforce their role in their families. We see the role in several ways:

The reputation—We usually hear about their reputation long before we get to know them. Their families and friends are usually glad to tell us about it—out of Christian love, of course.

The convincing role—Scapegoats have bought into the image they've acquired. They crave acceptance and affection, but they can't get either in their family. So they settle for getting attention—which negative behavior certainly draws. That attention is better than nothing, Scapegoats reason, so they give in to their roles. And they play them convincingly.

The unacceptable behavior—Finally, Scapegoats often act out their feelings in unacceptable ways—bullying, stealing, using drugs or alcohol, being sexually promiscuous. They bring trouble and stress to youth groups. This trouble confirms the reputation which preceded them. We say, "Well, this is what people said to expect."

While Scapegoats rarely come to youth group meetings, you'll often see their families in juvenile detention centers or court. Or the parents may ask you to "straighten the kid out" through counseling.

In each instance, our first instinct may be to assume—like everyone else—that the teenager is the root of the problem. The kid fell in with the wrong crowd or is running from God or is just plain mean-spirited. But when you meet a Scapegoat, ask yourself: "What's going on in the Scapegoat's life to encourage the troublesome behavior? Could the family, despite all public appearances, be alcoholic or in some other way troubled?"

The Scapegoat's needs—The unconditional acceptance we offer all group members will be especially meaningful to Scapegoats. They substitute *attention* for the *acceptance* they crave.

Unconditional acceptance doesn't mean accepting the Scapegoats' negative behaviors. However, these teenagers may not believe such a distinction is possible, since they're used to the image of being only as good as the bad things they do. Yet Scapegoats need to know nothing they do can make you love them less, just like Family Heroes need to know nothing they do can make you love them more.

More Alike Than Different

On the outside, all of these young people have learned to cope well with their situations. A few even appear to be well-adjusted teenagers. But when we peek behind their masks, we see something else. We're shocked and saddened by the pain they withstand. And though the Family Hero, Lost Child, Mascot and Scapegoat may seem completely different, they're strikingly similar:

They're unnoticed. If you'd met a Hero and a Scapegoat before reading the descriptions, which would you have identified as the typical child of an alcoholic? Most people would answer the Scapegoat. But that's a misperception.

In her book *It Will Never Happen to Me!*, Dr. Black writes how surprised she was to learn that many children of alcoholics don't fit the image fixed in her mind. They aren't runaways or chemical abusers. They don't get into trouble with the law or with school authorities. They aren't under-achievers. In short, many don't fit the Scapegoat stereotype.

"While there is a substantial number of problematic children from alcoholic homes," Dr. Black writes, "the majority of these children simply do not draw enough attention to themselves to even be identified as being in need of special attention. They are a neglected population. If they are busy and look good, they will be ignored."[7]

I can relate to her perceptions. I was a combination of the Family Hero and the Mascot. My predominant role, by far, was the Hero. But if that didn't work, the Mascot would try some one-liners to defuse a problem. Because I looked good, kept incredibly busy and seemed to have my life together, nobody suspected a problem. Or at least no one said anything.

Many children of alcoholics go unnoticed for the same reason. They play roles to look good and be accepted. They fit so well in our society and churches that we can't believe they're hurting. Only Scapegoats get our attention—by making their anger and pain noticeable.

They have similar emotional experiences and needs. Because of the "don't feel" rule, children of alcoholics rarely identify and accept their feelings. But when they begin healing, they frequently name at least five basic feelings that plagued them as children and teenagers: anger, fear, guilt, sadness and worthlessness.

Though masks hide them, these feelings eat away at young people's esteem and sense of purpose. It doesn't matter which survival role kids play; the role merely helps them cope with their emotions.

I recently heard an adult child of an alcoholic describe his childhood. "I can remember experiencing happiness once for about 20 minutes," he said. "I've spent my life since trying to feel that again." How tragic that the primary emotions children of alcoholics experience are negative.

Without help, each will continue to struggle. The problems children of alcoholics face result from continuing to live by the alcoholic family rules and the survival roles. COAs become emotionally and spiritually frozen in childhood, when they were victims who needed the rules and roles just to survive. They take their alcoholic family rules and roles into adulthood where they use them as the foundation for all relationships. As a result, the problems they fled actually follow them, reincarnating the unhealthy patterns.

This delayed reaction is one reason why we must act to move the child toward healing and recovery while he or she is still in the family. Most children of alcoholics will appear to be coping. But we shouldn't trust this image until time and experience have confirmed it.

Adult children of alcoholics counselor Earnie Larsen describes the phenomenon with this formula:

What you live with, you learn.

What you learn, you practice.

What you practice, you become.[8]

I extend this formula one line and one generation further:

What you become, you pass on.

Larsen's formula summarizes the frightful future facing teenagers from alcoholic families. After years of living with survival rules and roles, they no longer know their true selves. They become the roles they act, and they play by the only rules they know.

And survival becomes their lifestyle.

This survival lifestyle shows up in the strangest ways. The "Traits of Adult Children of Alcoholics" box on page 62 lists some of the characteristics that children of alcoholics often carry to adulthood if they don't receive help. Other characteristics make funny, though insightful, stories.

My dad frequently experienced blackouts from drinking. He'd lose his memory, but not his consciousness. He

Traits of Adult Children of Alcoholics

When children of alcoholics leave their alcoholic homes, they don't leave behind the patterns they learned. If they don't overcome the unhealthy patterns learned while children and teenagers, those patterns will haunt them throughout their lives. Some of the patterns include:

- Difficulty following through with projects

- Difficulty playing and having fun

- Overreacting to changes over which they have no control

- Lying when it's just as easy to tell the truth

- Being overly self-critical and self-judgmental

- Taking themselves seriously, even when they're being funny

- Difficulty establishing and maintaining intimate relationships

- Feeling starved for approval and affirmation

- Being either super-responsible or super-irresponsible

- Seeking immediate gratification of wants and needs

- Committing to a particular course of action without seriously considering other possibilities or the action's consequences

- Seeking out (or even creating) tension or crisis, then complaining about the results[9]

could do almost anything but never remember it later.

This made him dangerous in the kitchen. On three occasions Dad put a pan on the range, turned on the burner and forgot about it. He started a small fire at least once this way. Mom extinguished it before it set the house aflame, but it was a close call.

Being the Family Hero, I started checking the range before I left the house or before I went to bed. As Dad's drinking progressed, so did my addiction to Heroism. Soon I didn't stop with the range. I checked every electrical appliance in the kitchen. I unplugged the toaster, coffeemaker, blender and radio. Anything that could theoretically cause an electrical fire became a hazard that needed to be unplugged.

After a time, my unplugging went beyond the kitchen. I unplugged the television, stereo and lamps in the living room. And I no longer checked these electrical threats just once. I'd check them twice, three times and even more. At night I'd wait until my dad went to bed, then I'd get up and check one last time.

When I got married, guess what little gift I brought my wife? Besides my Hero costume, I kept my compulsive habit. I don't know how much time Lynne spent waiting in our car while I unplugged small appliances before we could go anywhere. And it became terribly aggravating for her to find untoasted bread in the toaster when we sat down for breakfast.

I could never explain my obsession until I began to understand myself as an adult child of an alcoholic. A counselor asked me to write my life history. He told me to discuss with him any concern or insight that came to me while I was writing. I decided to mention my bizarre ritual.

After listening to my story, he explained that I had become obsessed with caring for my father. Realizing that Dad didn't always have a clear mind, I had begun to watch over him. The checking had become an automatic behavior—whether it was needed or not. It wasn't needed now because my wife was fully capable of turning off the range.

But there was another reason my behavior was no longer needed. "Tom, your dad's dead now," the counselor said. "You don't have to take care of him anymore."

I can't explain those words' impact. I knew Dad was dead. I'd been at his bedside when he died and at his funeral three days later. Yet he still lived in the kitchen of my mind. And I still had to follow him around to make sure he didn't start a fire.

Beyond Recognition

You may wonder what adult children of alcoholics have to do with youth ministry. After all, you deal with teenagers, not adults.

Yet the connection between teenagers in alcoholic families and the adults they will become is vital. Why? Because so many of the hurts that are hidden in childhood and adolescence become unbearably painful in adulthood.

This delayed reaction easily tricks us into a lethargic attitude toward teenage COAs in our church. We see them and say: "They look all right. They seem normal. They must be handling it okay." But remember, that's what they want us to see! It's the image they've created with the family rules and roles. And when we buy into the deception without considering the long-range consequences, these teenagers fall through the cracks of our ministries.

Inside teenagers from alcoholic families are wounded people who hope someone will see them as they really are. They need people who will dare to peek behind the masks they wear.

Yet looking without offering help would be worse than not looking at all. The next section suggests ways to do more than just look.

Work It Out

1. Quickly review the stories of children of alcoholics in the opening of this chapter and in previous chapters. Identi-

Roles in My Youth Group

Instructions: In the space beside each role, write the names of kids in your youth group you identify with that role. Remember, not all group members will come from alcoholic families. But each teenager may still have particular role tendencies.

Once you've completed the list, review the names beside each role. Place a checkmark by the name of each teenager you suspect may live in an alcoholic or otherwise troubled family.

Finally, review the list of checkmarked names. Based on your experience and knowledge of the families, circle those presently facing the most imminent risks.

Role	Group Members Who May Play This Role
Family Hero	
Lost Child	
Mascot	
Scapegoat	

fy each child according to the roles presented in this chapter (Family Hero, Lost Child, Mascot, Scapegoat).

2. Fill out the "Roles in My Youth Group" chart on page 65.

3. Select one "high risk" teenager from each section in the chart. Brainstorm ways you could make each aware of the need for assistance. Keep in mind the survival rules each uses, as well as the unique role each plays in the family. Read the remaining chapters in this book for guidelines or healthy intervention and support.

Endnotes

[1]Charles Leerhsen, "Alcohol and the Family," Newsweek (January 18, 1988), 68.

[2]Claudia Black, It Will Never Happen to Me! (Denver, CO: M.A.C. Communications, 1981).

[3]Black, It Will Never Happen to Me! 14.

[4]Sharon Wegscheider-Cruse, Choice-Making for Co-Dependents, Adult Children and Spirituality Seekers (Pompano Beach, FL: Health Communications, 1985), 41.

[5]Charles Deutsch, Broken Bottles, Broken Dreams: Understanding and Helping the Children of Alcoholics (New York: Teachers College Press, 1982), 41.

[6]Wegscheider-Cruse, Choice-Making for Co-Dependents, Adult Children and Spirituality Seekers, 41.

[7]Black, It Will Never Happen to Me! 15-16.

[8]Earnie Larsen, For Adult Children of Alcoholics and Those Who Love Them (audio tape series), (Brooklyn Park, MN: E. Larsen Enterprises, 1984).

[9]Janet G. Woititz, Adult Children of Alcoholics (Pompano Beach, FL: Health Communications, 1983), 4-5.

PART 2

Healing the Wounds

CHAPTER 5

Nice Help or Healthy Help?

How Our Efforts Can Do More Harm Than Good

Once we admit that our youth groups include children of alcoholics, the implications become overwhelming. We want to help. But we don't know how. And often our attempts at helping show that all "help" is not necessarily helpful.

Any parent with an inquisitive toddler knows this. After a late-summer thunderstorm I began to repair a storm-damaged door. I laid out the tools I'd need and started to work.

Then my toddler son decided to "help." Each time I needed a different tool, I had to coax it from Jake. Usually he'd resist. He needed it, he'd say. Twice I barely averted additional repair jobs when I spotted him "fixing" a newly painted wall with a hammer. And when I needed screws or washers, I first had to find them—under a rug, inside snow boots or in crevices in the stairway.

Though Jake's assistance made for a wonderful father-and-son adventure, it also complicated the job. His well-intentioned help turned a simple 30-minute job into a complex hour-long task.

Jake's help was nice—but not really helpful.

The same could describe the help churches usually give kids from alcoholic families. We want to help, but our efforts may do more harm than good. Junie's story illustrates.

Junie's Story

Unlike Jerry in Chapter 1, Junie wasn't the kind of teenager who's easy to have in a youth group. Generally, she was difficult at group meetings, frequently in trouble at school and always at odds with her parents. Each time, the problem was the same. At 15 going on 25, Junie attracted any guy, and she encouraged and accepted his attention. If no one appeared interested, she took it as a personal challenge to create interest.

Junie's reputation for wild passion and loose morals was reinforced by taunting classmates. They'd say you could always tell when the school was having a home game by the suggestive way Junie dressed. Rumor had it that her pre- and post-game "shows" were known throughout the conference.

Junie didn't come from a "bad" family. Her parents were respected community and church leaders. They lived comfortably yet modestly in what appeared to be a happy, stable and church-oriented home.

The youth staff frequently encouraged Junie's parents to get professional help for their daughter. But they never did. They said they preferred to trust in God to see them—and her—through the problem. They said they believed the promise of Proverbs 22:6 that Junie would turn around because they had raised her "in the way she should go."

Privately the youth leaders joked about Junie's fascination with guys. Before group outings to the malls, they'd remind each other to keep a close watch on Junie around the male mannequins. Over soft drinks they'd speculate about Junie's future career. Would she be a "boy scout"? A "male carrier"? A men's room attendant? Maybe she'd become an anthropologist who would discover a hidden all-male society.

One Saturday afternoon in late winter, Sheila—a youth leader—received a call from a youth group member. Marcie was calling on behalf of Junie who had spent the night. They needed to talk to Sheila. Within an hour the three were together.

Marcie started the conversation. Junie had come to her house after midnight, Marcie explained, and asked for a place to stay. Junie was distraught and crying, and the left side of her face was red and slightly swollen. With her mother's permission Marcie made a bed for Junie. They didn't talk then, but Marcie held Junie while she sobbed into a fitful sleep.

By morning Junie's face was swollen and bruised. After breakfast she told Marcie what had happened. It took several hours for Marcie to convince Junie they should tell Sheila.

Then, slowly and haltingly, Junie started to talk through her tears—but only after Marcie's whispered encouragement. Friday night Junie had returned home from a ball game to find her father drunk as usual.

"What do you mean by 'as usual'?" Sheila asked.

Junie explained that each Friday night for as long as she could remember, her father would bring home booze and drink until drunk. Shocked by this information, Sheila challenged Junie by asking her why she had never seen any evidence of her dad's drinking on Sunday morning.

"You've never been to our house on Friday night," Junie replied. "And he sleeps it off on Saturday."

Junie continued her story. She came home last night to find her parents fighting. When her mother grabbed the bottle and began pouring it out in the sink, her father began to beat her mother. When he slammed her against a wall, Junie tried to intervene, and her father's anger turned on her. He pinned Junie against the wall and began to scream over and over at her: "Filthy bitch! Filthy bitch!"

To get away, she tried to kick him in the groin. But her blow missed, and his rage became insane. Holding her against the wall with his left hand, he struck her repeatedly in the face with his right. After several blows Junie managed to struggle free and bolt from the house. She ran straight to Marcie's.

By the time Junie finished her story, both she and Marcie were in tears. Sheila was dumbfounded, her mind whirling. Could this be true? She knew Junie's parents, didn't she? Should she believe Junie—this girl who had a history of lying to cover her sexual adventures? Yet Junie was reporting serious abuse. Should Sheila report it? What if it wasn't true? What if Junie was just trying to get back at her parents for their discipline? What if it was just another wild story?

Finally Sheila decided to talk with Junie's parents. When she told Junie how she'd help, Junie became hysterical. She begged Sheila not to talk with them, not to tell them she had told. But the stronger Junie protested, the stronger Sheila's suspicions became. After calming Junie by telling her everything would work out, Sheila drove to Junie's home.

Junie's mother looked tired and stressed when she greeted Sheila at the door. After taking Sheila into the living room, she excused herself to get Junie's dad. When the mother returned, Sheila awkwardly made small talk until the father arrived—nearly half an hour later. He had been working on the car, he explained, and needed to clean up before coming in.

As Sheila told them Junie's story, they reacted with surprise, anger and tears. The mother sobbed, and the father offered to tell the true story.

Junie had come home from the ball game after curfew with the facial injury, he began. When he asked about her reddened face, she refused to talk. Yes, a family argument did follow. But he never laid a hand on her. Eventually, he said, Junie admitted she'd been beaten by a boy she picked up at the game.

Junie's dad confessed to Sheila that he had become furious with his daughter. In his anger he told her she had a choice: either clean up her life or get out. Junie screamed obscenities at him and went out the door. She came back shortly only to tell them she'd spend the night at Marcie's. Since they knew she was at Marcie's they hadn't been concerned.

Throughout his explanation, he held his wife's hand and slowly stroked it. His wife gently sobbed and stared at the floor.

The father concluded by asking Sheila to keep them in her thoughts and prayers. This, he said, was typical of what they'd come to expect with Junie. It was just another example of her rebellion, and it showed that she was a sick girl and needed the help only God could provide.

Sheila prayed with the stricken parents before she left. And she prayed for herself as she drove away. She felt confused, and decided she needed other people's counsel.

The next day, she asked the other youth leaders and the pastor to meet with her after the Sunday morning service. She told the two stories and awaited their suggestions. After considerable discussion, the group decided to accept the parents' version. It probably wasn't the whole truth, but it certainly seemed more reasonable than Junie's tale. The group also discussed several responses and decided to reunite the family and insist that Junie receive professional counseling.

Within two weeks of the reunion Junie ran away from home. She was gone for more than two months before she was found. Upon her return, she was placed in a group home for troubled kids.

Almost two years later, after a violent drinking episode that sent her mother fleeing to a shelter for battered spouses, Junie's dad entered an alcoholism treatment center. The ensuing months of therapy resulted in full confirmation of Junie's story.

Junie is now in her mid-20s. She's in therapy for sexual addiction. She's also in a support group for adult children of alcoholics. Junie sometimes sees her mother, but never her father. And she believes the only good purpose for churches is to provide dry, warm places for weddings and funerals.

Sheila struggles with a bad case of the "if onlys." If only she'd believed Junie's story. If only she'd not made Junie go back. Maybe things would be different. Friends have counseled her to stop beating herself. She did the best she knew how. Yet the pain of her guilt speaks louder than their kind words.

Help That Isn't Helpful

Sheila's struggle with guilt is similar to the guilt people frequently feel after giving what I call "Nice Help." Though Nice Help grows out of the best of motives and attitudes, it often complicates and extends alcoholic families' unnecessary pain.

Let's look at some characteristics of this Nice Help:

Nice Help avoids discomfort. If doctors were Nice Help givers, they'd never give injections or operate on a patient. The needles and scalpels hurt too much.

Nice Help givers want to heal without conflict, confrontation or discomfort—even when essential for healing. This unrealistic approach robs the Nice Help giver of a truly healing tool: truth. The Nice Help giver rarely speaks the truth unless it's easy to speak.

Sheila wasn't willing to confront Junie's parents about the possibility of conflict in their home. Instead, she opted for the easy "healing" by believing the parents' seemingly less-painful diagnosis.

Nice Help means well. For Nice Help givers, sincerity is everything. They try hard to help, even when the person refuses help. As a result, Nice Help givers often become physically, emotionally and spiritually drained. Convinced their sincere effort should make a difference, they're shocked when it doesn't. And they often blame the one they're trying to help.

Nice Help blames the victim. "Did you do something to provoke the fight?" "What role do you have in all this?" "What can you do differently to improve the situation?"

Why do Nice Helpers ask these kinds of things? Maybe they don't know anything else to say. Maybe the victim's story is difficult to believe. Or maybe they just want to find a quick, easy solution with the least amount of inconvenience, conflict and confrontation.

In any case, the result is the same. It reinforces one of the most devastating, erroneous ideas held by the victim: that he or she really is responsible for the problem.

Nice Help determines its actions based on the helper's assumptions, not the victim's needs. When Sheila tried to help, she drew upon her own assumptions about Junie's situation. These were, in turn, confirmed by members of the church's ministry team. Sadly, everyone assumed Junie wasn't being honest. The Nice Help that resulted merely kept Junie and her mother in a dangerous, abusive home, while protecting her father from the truth about himself. It actually prolonged the family's pain.

Such is the nature of Nice Help. Nice Help givers respond to needs based on their perceptions or assumptions. Their blinders shield their eyes from the wounds that need healing.

Help That Is Helpful

As Sheila learned, Nice Help is terribly inadequate for children of alcoholic families. Good intentions and sincerity are not enough. The help we give must be a "Healthy Help" that truly offers healing to these families.

Providing Healthy Help is a formidable challenge that involves several emphases:

Healthy Help involves loving God and myself before I can love someone else. I entered the ministry determined to base my work on a veteran youth worker's dictum: "Burn out, don't rust out!" Not only did I live by this principle, I followed it. I burned out.

I never would have burned out if my model had been Jesus Christ. He didn't teach his followers to follow that dictum. In fact, he challenged this concept, which was being taught by the Pharisees—the compulsive perfectionists of his day. Jesus taught us: " 'Love the Lord your God with all your heart and with all your soul and with all your mind.' This is the first and greatest commandment. And the second is like it: 'Love your neighbor as yourself.' " (Matthew 22:37-39).

This saying of Jesus is both simple and profound. On one level, it challenges me to examine my love for myself, then to give no less than the same to others.

On another level, it gives me a glimpse of how my self-love affects the love I give. If I have a healthy, nurturing, freeing love for myself, then I'll give a healthy, nurturing, freeing love to others. If, on the other hand, my self-love is sickly, repressive and selfish, those traits will characterize my love for others.

Teenagers from alcoholic families need a model of healthy self-love. While different children of alcoholics take different roles in the family, each still suffers from low self-esteem. Thus each needs to learn healthy self-love.

Healthy Help is giving help to others while God is helping me and healing my wounds. Henri Nouwen's book *The Wounded Healer: Ministry in Contemporary Society* has meant a lot to me and my ministry. Nouwen pictures the minister as a wounded healer who "must look after his own wounds but at the same time be prepared to heal the wounds of others . . . He is both the wounded minister and the healing minister."[1]

Nouwen's words echo the Apostle Paul in 2 Corinthians 12:7-10. Paul tells how God works through him because of—not in spite of—his wounds. He quotes Jesus' words that "my grace is sufficient for you, for my power is made perfect in weakness." Paul was so comfortable relying on Christ's power that he determined gladly to boast of his weaknesses in order that "Christ's power may rest on me."

We accomplish more with children of alcoholics if we admit our weaknesses and wounds than if we glorify our strengths. Of course, ministering out of our weaknesses involves first being aware of and admitting those wounds.

That's not always easy.

I recently attended a youth worker fellowship. Two strong feelings confronted me during the meeting. First, I felt old. At 34, I was the oldest person in the group. The second feeling resulted from the tension I felt in the room. I wasn't sure what caused the tension at first. Then I noted how everyone seemed so "right"—not in the sense of correct or incorrect, but in the sense of image. Everyone talked right, acted right, dressed right. It felt like the youth workers were meeting to compare spit-shines and encourage one another to keep up the image.

My impression from that meeting illustrates a pervasive problem in ministry, particularly youth ministry: the image of the superhuman minister.

However, teenagers from alcoholic families will never respond as well to the "right" image as they will to the wounded youth worker. When we deny our need for healing, our ministry suffers. We come across as super-righteous, perfect and Godlike. Those who hurt feel afraid to approach us because their need seems to be much greater in our presence.

When we admit our wounds and weaknesses, we open ourselves to a whole flood of fresh experiences. In our vulnerability, others become more vulnerable with us. We experience God's grace as he heals us and uses our brokenness to heal others. Our ministries take on new power through our admission of powerlessness. "For when I am weak, then I am strong" (2 Corinthians 12:10).

Healthy Help loves enough to let people make their own choices. I have trouble letting people have their own way. For as long as I can remember I've been a "take charge" or controlling person. This characteristic makes it difficult to accept Jesus' ministry style. He loved and respected people enough to let them choose their responses to him. His encounter with the wealthy young man illustrates his style.

Now a man came up to Jesus and asked, "Teacher,

what good thing must I do to get eternal life?"

"Why do you ask me about what is good?" Jesus replied. "There is only One who is good. If you want to enter life, obey the commandments."

"Which one?" the man inquired.

Jesus replied, " 'Do not murder, do not commit adultery, do not steal, do not give false testimony, honor your father and mother,' and 'love your neighbor as yourself.' "

"All these I have kept," the young man said. "What do I still lack?"

Jesus answered, "If you want to be perfect, go, sell your possessions and give to the poor, and you will have treasure in heaven. Then come, follow me."

When the young man heard this, he went away sad, because he had great wealth (Matthew 19:16-22).

What stands out is not what Jesus said or did, but what he *didn't* say or do. Simply, Jesus didn't cajole the man to try. He didn't adjust the standards to make following him easier. And he didn't try to lessen the man's sadness. He let him walk away in pain.

If I had been with Jesus as he talked with the young man, I would have protested as soon as the man moved from earshot. "What in the world are you doing, Lord?" I might have asked. "Can't you see this guy is hurting? He really wants to follow you. Give him a chance! In time he'll cut loose from his bucks." Maybe that's what the disciples were thinking when they asked, "Who then can be saved?"

The church isn't comfortable letting people struggle. We step in to give the answer or to help or to take responsibility. But this well-intentioned Nice Help actually hurts. It insulates people from the working of God's Spirit.

One way we keep people from making their own choices is by "meddling." Christians are great meddlers— even though we may call it "caring," "ministering," "being concerned," "helping" or even "pastoring." Though these names certainly denote legitimate actions, we sometimes reduce the actions to meddling. And, in reality, meddling is a subtle form of denying people their own right to choose.

Meddling violates what God himself won't violate: our free wills. To give Healthy Help, we too must honor each person's God-given freedom. We can't force ourselves or our well-intentioned help on anyone who doesn't want to receive it. Like Jesus, we must acknowledge that the decision to receive help is born out of a sense of need and pain.

Perhaps the role of pain in moving people to receive help can be better understood in the context of a dental appointment. Do I go to the dentist when I have only a tiny, tolerable periodic pain? Of course not! I won't face the dentist until it's a horrible, throbbing, face-numbing pain. When my pain overshadows my fear, I run to the office, force my way ahead of the other patients, leap into the chair and beg the dentist to start pulling.

When we give Healthy Help, we let people retain their freedom to choose. Many times they will choose pain—even when we have explained to them that it's unnecessary. We'll pity them. We'll be tempted to help them, even forcibly. But unless they've said yes to our help, we must not act.

This aspect of Healthy Help is critical in working with kids of alcoholics and their families. This detachment (as Al-Anon groups call it) doesn't mean we stop caring. It means we care enough to let people make their own choices. Healthy Help is a powerful tool, though it seems at first to be unkind. If we're accustomed to giving Nice Help, it's difficult to stop meddling and to start practicing detachment.

Healthy Help knows the difference between myself and God. Early in my own recovery as an adult child of an alcoholic, I attended an Al-Anon meeting I won't easily forget. After the introductions, the leader let people comment on the session's topic: spirituality. A woman across the room from me spoke up. Her comment was brief and profound. She said, "The most important thing I need to know about God is that I'm not him."

For most of my life I have been on a God-trip. It wasn't intentional or conscious. Yet I lived in the confusion of where God left off and I began. No challenge was too great. I could cure any ill, save any soul, mend any break. I felt powerful, and it felt good.

But the awful flip side was the feeling of heavy responsibility. If I wasn't there, who would do it? If I didn't know about the hurt, how could I heal it? If I fixed someone but they fell apart again, wasn't it my fault? After all, my work was guaranteed.

Healthy Helpers can't guarantee anything. They don't have all the answers. They clearly know their limitations as helpers. And one of the healthiest helping responses is to cooperate with others who can offer more effective help to the victims of alcoholism.

Knowing we're not God appropriately ties together all aspects of Healthy Help. We give our best love to God and allow him to establish the other love priorities of our life. We have permission to be human and to admit our wounds. We can liberate others to make their own choices. And, as a result, we become God's channels of Healthy Help to the teenagers in our groups, their parents, our friends, our peers and our family.

The Move From Nice to Healthy Help

While it's easy to understand the difference between Nice and Healthy Help in other people, it's sometimes difficult to see it in ourselves. We must personalize the issue by asking ourselves: Which am I? A Nice Help giver? Or a Healthy Help giver?

Use the "Is Your Help Helpful?" quiz on page 81 to begin this self-evaluation process. (It might be helpful to ask a trusted friend to help you.)

After you've finished, ask yourself which helping pattern seems most dominant in your ministry:

● Does my score accurately represent my own helping style? Why or why not?

● What traps do I see in my own personality that can lead to Nice Help instead of Healthy Help?

Is Your Help Helpful?

Respond to each of the 10 statements by checking the appropriate box.

	Always	Usually	Seldom	Never
1. I take adequate time each week just for myself.	☐	☐	☐	☐
2. I work hard to keep peace in all my relationships.	☐	☐	☐	☐
3. I can give problems and concerns to God without worrying or fretting about them.	☐	☐	☐	☐
4. I suspect a ''con job'' when a group member tells me a hard-to-believe story or problem.	☐	☐	☐	☐
5. I can let others do as they want even if I personally disagree with their choice.	☐	☐	☐	☐
6. I am good at assessing teenagers' problems and can quickly give advice.	☐	☐	☐	☐
7. I know when I need help and ministry from others, and will receive it from them.	☐	☐	☐	☐
8. I don't give up on people's problems, and I won't let them give up.	☐	☐	☐	☐
9. I can openly, appropriately and freely express my opinions, ideas and feelings.	☐	☐	☐	☐
10. I feel depressed when a kid I've tried to help fails to resolve his or her problem.	☐	☐	☐	☐

continued

Assessing Your Response
Total your responses in the following chart:

	Always or Usually	Seldom or Never
Odd-numbered statements		
Even-numbered statements		

● If you chose mainly "always" and "usually" responses on the *odd*-numbered statements and mainly "seldom" and "never" responses on the *even*-numbered statements, you're probably a Healthy Help giver.

● If you chose mainly "usually" and "always" responses on the *even*-numbered statements—regardless of how you responded on the odd-numbered ones—you're probably a Nice Help giver.

● If your responses don't fall into one of these patterns, you probably have some Nice Help tendencies to work on, but you also have some characteristics of Healthy Help.

● What are specific ways to overcome some of the Nice Help patterns I've developed?

● What examples of Nice Help and Healthy Help have I seen in my own church and ministry?

If you find that you tend toward Nice Help, you are—in essence—functioning as a co-dependent in relation to your youth group. Take these practical steps to begin dealing with the tendency:

● Find and attend a Co-dependents Anonymous or Al-Anon group in your area. These groups will help you learn more about Nice versus Healthy Help (though they won't use these terms). More important, they'll teach you the key concepts of Healthy Help.

● Talk to a counselor experienced in helping people deal with co-dependency.

● Study Edwin Friedman's book, *Generation to Gener-*

ation: Family Process in Church and Synagogue.[2] This book provides a comprehensive guide for church workers who want to give truly helpful and healing leadership to their congregations. It will also help you better understand healthy and unhealthy functioning in individual families and your congregation.

The transition to Healthy Help isn't easy—especially in a church that is strongly predisposed toward Nice Help. But the transition is essential. It results in greater inner peace as you really offer your youth group the most effective kind of help.

Work It Out

1. In addition to the characteristics of Nice Help listed in the chapter, what other characteristics can you think of? What are other characteristics of Healthy Help?

2. Read "Melinda's Family" on page 84. This case study, which is based on a true situation, illustrates how difficult it can be to determine the healthiest response. Struggle with the story, and answer the following questions:

● If you say yes, how would it help Melinda? hurt her?

● If you say no, how would it help her? hurt her?

● Which seems the healthiest response for Melinda's sake? Why?

● Which seems the healthiest response for you? Why?

● What is the most loving response you could make? Explain.

There's no perfect answer for how to respond to Melinda's request. Here's one response—though it may not always be the most appropriate response:

Realizing the danger of giving Nice Help by not challenging Melinda to take responsibility for herself, you could say, "I'm sorry your home situation is difficult, and I know you can't control your parents. But we had an agreement last time that you could control. I'm willing to help you this time, but only if you commit to at least four Alateen meetings. If you don't, it wouldn't be good for you for me to continue to bail you out."

3. How can you know the difference between healthy self-love and unhealthy self-centeredness?

4. Does vulnerability have any limits? Explain your position.

5. Do you agree or disagree with the following statement? "When a person experiences a divine calling to youth work, that call also carries a divine right to interpret God's will in the lives of others." Explain your answer.

6. When do you think it's appropriate to "step in" and make decisions for other people? What guidelines would you offer for yourself and your ministry?

Melinda's Family

Melinda is a regular in your youth group. It's no secret that Melinda's dad is a binge drinker. About once every two months he spends a weekend—and a whole paycheck—in a bar.

This means a tough two weeks for Melinda's family. Her family usually gets by on the extra cash her mom hides between binges to make sure she can meet all the necessary expenses.

But on one occasion the binge happened just before a youth group retreat Melinda had signed up to attend. Melinda sheepishly came to request a scholarship for the retreat. She explained that the family had enough money to pay basic family expenses, but not enough to cover her retreat fee. She asked if you would help her.

You took the opening with Melinda to discuss her father's alcoholism. And hoping to move Melinda and her family toward healing, you agreed to pay her fee from the ample scholarship fund if she agreed to attend weekly Alateen meetings for one month. Melinda readily agreed. She attended the retreat, but only two Alateen meetings.

Now she's back and broke again. Her father has been on another drinking binge. Melinda owes you money for a ticket to a concert tomorrow night. She can't pay because money is short at home. She really wants to go to the concert with the rest of the group. Could you—would you—pay for her ticket from the scholarship fund?

Endnotes

[1]Henri Nouwen, *The Wounded Healer: Ministry in Contemporary Society* (Garden City, NY: Doubleday, 1979), 82.

[2]Edwin H. Friedman, *Generation to Generation: Family Process in Church and Synagogue* (New York: Guilford Press, 1985).

CHAPTER 6

Where Is the Church?

How the Church Can Help, But Often Hurts, Alcoholic Families

No other institution within society can help alcoholic
families more than the church. But—with the exception
of the liquor industry—probably no other institution has
done more harm to alcoholic families than the church.

I've wrestled with writing that paragraph for almost a
year. When I see it on paper, it seems harsh and critical.
The second statement might make you think I'm against the
church. But I'm not. I continue to work within the church
and through the church, because I firmly believe the first
sentence: The church *can* do more for alcoholic families
than any other institution. I believe this for three basic
reasons:

● The church has a solution for the alcoholic family's
dilemma. Alcoholics Anonymous views alcoholism as a
problem "which only a spiritual experience will conquer."[1]
Where better than the church could an alcoholic family seek
a spiritual solution?

● The church is seen as a healing place. Like any other hurting family, the alcoholic family seeks something to take its pain away. Its members are driven by an unconscious yearning to remove—or at least numb—their pain. They perceive the church as a place where they can realize this hope. For this reason many children of alcoholics already come to us.

● The church has access to the deepest reaches of personal and family life. No one else in our culture has such license, even responsibility, to ask tough personal questions and to expect answers. Pastors, youth workers and other ministers have an especially unique role in our society. And they have unparalleled access to a place most people can never go: into other people's homes. This gift of accessibility is a powerful tool for helping alcoholic families.

A few congregations have developed significant ministries to alcoholics and their families by emphasizing these characteristics. However, the church, as a whole, has done more harm than good by giving Nice Help instead of Healthy Help. Let's look at some evidence.

Honesty and Denial

To exist, alcoholism must have an environment that's humid with dishonesty. Thus, above all else, alcoholic families need honesty to recover and maintain health and growth. Without this honesty, families never cut through the layers of self-deception that allow the alcoholism to flourish.

In *People of the Lie: The Hope for Healing Human Evil*, Dr. M. Scott Peck describes people who are most easily helped by psychotherapy. They are the most honest. In contrast, the most difficult people to help are the most dishonest. Indeed, Peck believes they're nearly beyond help and hope—until they clarify their thinking and become honest in their behavior.[2]

Unfortunately, the church is often a greenhouse where dishonesty thrives. When I first began my recovery as an adult child of an alcoholic, it was difficult to stay in the church. I simply couldn't handle the level of dishonesty I sensed. I felt I always had to put on my mask to conform to the expectations and images that pervade the church.

I've shared my discomfort with other recovering adult children of alcoholics and addicts, and many of them have felt the same. Most churches don't welcome the "gut honesty" we learned about in recovery programs. As a result, recovering COAs may choose to leave the church for a while out of fear of falling back into unhealthy patterns that thrive in a dishonest environment.

Claudia told me of an experience in her Sunday school class that illustrates this discomfort. The class was studying the nature of God, and the discussion turned to comparing God with a loving parent. When asked for her ideas, Claudia admitted to the group she didn't like the image of God as parent and had difficulty relating to it. "When I imagine God as a parent," she explained, "all I can think of is my drunk mom screaming and swearing at me."

"Everyone froze," Claudia recalls. "They just stared at me." Finally the teacher spoke up. "That's pretty negative, Claudia," she said. "And it's not fair to God. Can you think of a more positive comment?" Claudia was stunned with disbelief. She simply said "no." The teacher said, "Thanks anyway, Claudia," and moved on to the next student. Claudia—who was trying to express herself honestly—felt alienated and humiliated by people who wouldn't allow such openness.

Let's look at some ways dishonesty invades the church and blocks opportunities to minister effectively to teenagers from alcoholic families:

Denial of alcoholism in the church—No corner of our culture is immune to alcoholism. Yet, though alcoholism is nearly epidemic in our country, many churches and youth workers still don't believe it's a problem in their congregation or denomination.

A friend of mine was asked to speak at a denominational conference. She could choose the topics. For one session she suggested "Helping Children of Alcoholics Through the

Sunday School." But the conference planners asked her to broaden the topic to include all kinds of troubled families. Not enough churches were facing problems of alcoholism, they said, to justify a whole workshop.

Not long ago I spoke to a group of more than 100 kids at a church camp. I told my story of growing up in an alcoholic family. And I asked each one to complete the "Children of Alcoholics Screening Test" (C.A.S.T.) (reprinted on page 114).

One out of every eight of these church kids recorded a score that undoubtedly pointed to alcoholism at home. One in eight—the same as the national ratio.

In order to help children of alcoholics, the church must first admit to the problem in its pews. By continuing to deny the problem, we hurt the most helpless victims even more. As long as we deny the presence of children of alcoholics in our churches, they:

- will remain unidentified.
- won't receive the support and nurture we can offer.
- will feel isolated because they don't feel "normal."
- will remain at risk of family violence.
- will themselves be likely candidates for addiction.
- will grow up to reproduce yet another generation of troubled people and unhealthy families.

Games Christians play—You may already know this game. I call it I'm Great, You're Great, That's Great! The game's object is to preserve your desired social image by keeping others from getting to know you too well. The rules are simple. Any time someone greets you with, "Hi! How are you doing?" you respond, "I'm great!"—regardless of how you really feel. The other person then responds, "Well, that's just great!" Then you exchange other meaningless pleasantries for a couple of minutes.

Recovering children of alcoholics are taught to be honest with their lives and feelings. A recovering COA actually tells how he or she feels, when asked, "How are you doing?" This strategy always loses in churches that play I'm Great, You're Great, That's Great!

Dr. Peck identifies the "People of the Lie" as evil people who hide their own evil from themselves. They become master deceivers, deceiving others and themselves. What do they look like? "We see the smile that hides the hatred, the smooth and oily manner that masks the fury, the velvet glove that covers the fist," Peck writes. "Because they are such experts at disguise, it is seldom possible to pinpoint the maliciousness of the evil."[3]

People of the Lie find a perfect hide-out in many churches. Indeed, Peck contends the church is one of the most common places for self-deceived people, because they are drawn to the disguise of piety.

Escapism—Our world can be a frightful place. Every day we see murder, rape, war, scandal, death and pain—courtesy of the evening news. Add to these problems job stress, family conflict, never-ending bills and other responsibilities of adulthood, and we all have plenty of reasons to look for escapes.

So we turn to the church.

There we hear about life on another plane. Life as a citizen in God's kingdom has real appeal. Our benevolent King will wipe our tears, heal our wounds, mend our broken hearts, calm our troubled spirits and even give us an eternity to enjoy perfect bodies in his presence.

There's nothing wrong with this good news. It's part of the gospel and the promise of abundant and eternal life (Luke 4:18-19 and Colossians 1:5, 23). It's a hope in God that must never be lost.

Yet this hope can be twisted into an unrealistic view of the world and our place in it. Instead of seeing the gospel as a hope that gives us vision and direction for life, we misuse the promise of a glorious eternity in heaven as an escape from the realities and responsibilities God has given us. And if we fall for the temptation to escape from life's realities, the consequences are profound.

● First, it puts us at odds with Jesus' teaching about our role in the world. In John 17:14-15 Jesus prays to the Father for his disciples: "I have given them your word and the world has hated them, for they are not of the world any more than I am of the world. My prayer is not that you take them out of the world but that you protect them from the evil one."

Recognizing our heavenly citizenship, Jesus only gives us "diplomatic immunity." He doesn't remove us. We still live in a place where people die, children are abused, scandals shake families, and people become alcoholic. While these things may not be okay, it's okay that we're here. Christ knows our situation. He wants us here to be his presence on Earth in the midst of the mess.

● The second consequence is that we begin interpreting events and circumstances according to how we'd like things to be rather than how they are. As a result, we deny the world's pain.

Jesus Christ knows the glories of God's kingdom better than anyone. Yet he chose to live in the moment. He didn't bemoan how things used to be. Nor did he sit around daydreaming about the future. He lived in the present, accepting people and circumstances as they were. He was fully available to others as a Healthy Helper.

When we reinterpret reality to fit our fantasy, we cross the line into dishonesty. We also begin to hurt ourselves and the alcoholic family because such wishful thinking parodies the patterns of alcoholic families.

Children of alcoholics constantly live in a fantasy world of "what could have been" or "what we hope will be." Their world is too painful to accept as reality. Some kids even create a fantasy family and life that they pass off as real. I call this the Cosby syndrome: The kids adopt Heathcliff and Clair Huxtable as their imaginary parents. The church seriously handicaps its efforts to help the alcoholic family if it shares such a fantasy.

And, with few exceptions, the church does propagate the myth in the fantasy of the "good Christian family." Particular traits of the good Christian family may vary from church to church, yet several ideals are held in common. Among them:

WHERE IS THE CHURCH? • **93**

1. Good Christian families have regular family devotions.

2. Good Christian families attend Sunday school and church every Sunday. (They still go when they're on vacation—even bringing home a bulletin to prove their faithfulness.) And *everyone* goes to church unless sick or dying.

3. Good Christian families rarely fight. And when they do, they fight lovingly. They never let a fight carry over into a new day.

4. Good Christian families teach their members not to bring disgrace or dishonor to the family. If a member deviates from good Christian behavior, it's a sign of rebellion against God. Intercessory prayer will bring the person to repentance and restoration with God.

5. Good Christian families will ultimately be known by their adult children's loyalty to the church.

When the "good Christian family" is the standard for all families, we reinforce the denial COAs maintain in order to keep the family secret. Or we quietly drive them from the church because of their sense of failure to meet the standard. In either case, we've missed an opportunity to help them.

Denying reality to maintain an image should have no place in the church. It only inflicts hurting people with a nagging pain that has no healing benefit.

Reduction of Alcoholism to a Moral Problem

At the heart of the church's discomfort with alcoholism may be a deeply held belief that addictions aren't real. The church has trouble accepting there are some things you can't overcome with willpower. As a result, arguing that some compulsive behaviors defy the standard religious remedies seems almost blasphemous to many Christians.

It's ironic, then, that one of the best descriptions of addiction comes from the Apostle Paul:

I do not understand what I do. For what I
want to do I do not do, but what I hate I do.
And if I do what I do not want to do, I agree

that the law is good. As it is, it is no longer I myself who do it, but it is sin living in me. I know
that nothing good lives in me, that is, in my sinful nature. For I have the desire to do what is
good, but I cannot carry it out. For what I do is
not the good I want to do; no, the evil I do not
want to do—this I keep on doing. Now if I do
what I do not want to do, it is no longer I who
do it, but it is sin living in me that does it. So I
find this law at work: When I want to do good,
evil is right there with me (Romans 7:15-21).

Paul happens to be writing about an addiction we call
"sin." Sin is something that infects the human race. It's
something we all do; its results are self-destructive; and it
can't be overcome apart from God's intervention. You might
say that sin is the greatest addiction of all.

If a person has lost the ability to choose whether he or
she even does something, that behavior is an addiction.
Regardless of the addiction, the desire to stop, while important, won't in itself deliver the captive.

The parallels between the power of sin and alcoholism
are profound. Most alcoholics want to stop drinking. They
may try hard not to drink, but they can't stop by sheer willpower. They may dry up for a few days—even weeks. But
they don't last. And each failed attempt results in greater
shame and guilt.

The cycle of alcoholism is the same cycle we each experience when we try to live the Christian life apart from
God's grace. Disgusted with our sinfulness, we vow to live
lives more pleasing to God. We try to be more devout and
more righteous. But we can't sustain it. We get tempted in
other directions, or we just tire of hanging on. In either
case, we blow it. Guilt and shame wrack us—making us feel
unworthy, useless and ashamed. Eventually—when we tire
of feeling shame—we muster the courage and determination
to try righteousness one more time. Thus we run in the
same circles as the alcoholic.

We escape from sin the same way alcoholics overcome their addiction. In Romans 7:24, Paul writes: "What a wretched man I am! Who will rescue me from this body of death? Thanks be to God—through Jesus Christ our Lord!" Deliverance comes only by God's grace. And it's through God's grace—not sheer willpower—that alcoholics stand their best chance of escaping their addiction.

The story of Bill W., co-founder of Alcoholics Anonymous, still inspires many alcoholics to begin recovery. He described what enabled him to break the alcoholic cycle in his own life:

> There I humbly offered myself to God, as I then understood Him, to do with me as He would. I placed myself unreservedly under His care and direction. I admitted for the first time that of myself I was nothing; that without Him I was lost. I ruthlessly faced my sins and became willing to have my new-found Friend take them away, root and branch. I have not had a drink since.[4]

Bill W. found release from his addiction by the experience of God's grace. Thus, alcoholics desperately need to hear the church's message of grace. Unfortunately, they often hear messages of condemnation instead.

Shame Instead of Responsibility

By condemning alcoholism as a moral weakness, churches compound the shame alcoholics feel about their uncontrollable addiction.

Let's be honest about the role of shaming in the church. In many instances, we use shame to move people to a commitment to Jesus Christ and our church. And we often use shame to pressure people to conform to our standards and accept our goals. In short, we use shame to control people.

It's important, at this point, to emphasize that the call for an end to shaming is not a call to ignore people's responsibilities. Shaming and calling people to responsibility are vastly different. While shaming is harmful, helping people understand their responsibility is helpful. In fact, part of recovery from alcoholism involves accepting responsibility for the behavior and its consequences. This is true for everyone caught in the alcoholic dilemma—the alcoholic, the spouse, the children.

This shaming hurts the alcoholic and the family in at least two ways:

Shaming turns people away. To shame is to confront people about their "bad" actions in such a way that insinuates they are "bad" people. As a result they feel "bad," and respond by doing what *we* want them to do (become a Christian or be a better Christian). While we may convince ourselves this manipulation builds God's kingdom—and ultimately helps alcoholics and their families—it doesn't always.

I believe shaming is *always* an inappropriate way to influence people. It destroys their self-esteem and diminishes the image of God within them. It manipulates them into changing outward actions, but it doesn't transform them inwardly.

Yet many churches use it because it appears to be effective. People who know right from wrong yet deliberately choose to do wrong are sometimes swayed by shame. So shame sometimes moves alcohol *abusers* to a higher plane of living. And since it's often difficult to tell the difference between an alcohol abuser and an alcohol addict, churches sometimes mistake success in shaming an abuser into temperance as success in curing an alcoholic.

But shaming has no positive effect on the true addict. When alcoholics see the pointed fingers and hear the shame flung by our churches, they usually retreat into the tranquility of the bottle. The alcohol plugs their ears to the condemnation they hear from without and feel from within. As a result, they leave the church and cut off opportunities for constructive, sensitive ministry.

This was Gerald's experience with the church. He knew he had a drinking problem. Shame and guilt took him to a church where he thought he'd find help. Gerald attended for several weeks, trying to work up the courage to tell the minister his story.

Just when he thought it was safe to talk without fear, the minister preached a scathing sermon on the moral problems of today. Drunkards were among the people the minister denounced as unworthy of God's grace and unrighteous for their lack of moral fiber. Gerald left the church never to return.

Shaming confirms the family's illusion of power. Everyone in the alcoholic family lives with an illusion of control. The alcoholic sincerely believes he or she can control the drinking. The spouse sincerely believes he or she can control the alcoholic. And the children sincerely believe they can, through their roles, control their parents' bizarre behavior. These illusions are often all that stands between the alcoholic family and healing help.

One reason for the "don't talk" rule in alcoholic families is that members think they ought to be able to deal with the problem alone. To take the problem to someone outside the family is like a confession of weakness. Families fear being looked down on because they couldn't handle their own problems.

However, instead of starving these illusions by emphasizing dependence on God's grace, the church feeds them with guilt trips.

Consider how the alcoholic family feels at First Church of the Holy Guilt Trip. Each week it hears how bad its behavior is, and each member feels bad. It hears it should buckle down and try harder so it'll be a good, alcohol-free Christian family. And each week the family leaves church making the quiet commitment, "This time it'll work!"

Sadly, this ideal lasts only until the alcoholic drinks again. Then each person is befuddled. "The church said I could change things," family members think to themselves. "Why didn't it work? Maybe God doesn't care . . . Sure he cares! Then why didn't he keep it from happening again? . . . Maybe he isn't powerful enough after all . . . No, that can't be true . . .

"Then it must be me. That's it! If only I could try harder or believe more or love God more. Then it would work.

"Oh, God, if only I had done better this time, it wouldn't have happened again. It's my fault. I'm no good."

Alcoholics Anonymous identifies the problem in the first step of its effective 12-Step recovery program: "We admitted we were powerless over alcohol—that our lives had become unmanageable." (For more on the 12-Step program, see page 134.) Anything the church does to reinforce the notion that alcoholics or their families can control the drinking will keep the families confined in their hell. Our shaming reinforces this deadly power delusion.

When Karla's family first began to face her mom's alcoholism, family members sought counsel from their pastor. In an attempt to help, the pastor tried to determine why the mother drank. He cited the father's frequent absences and his lack of spiritual leadership in the family as factors. Karla and her two sisters, the pastor suggested, might have contributed to the problem by the stress of their intense teenage schedules.

In response, Karla's dad took fewer work assignments out of town. He began leading the family in nightly devotions. Karla and her siblings cut back on their school activities.

But the mom still drank.

For a while, the family stayed with the counseling and tried each of the pastor's new suggestions. It finally became obvious that nothing they did or didn't do ever made a difference. Finally they stopped meeting with the pastor. Karla remembers the experience this way: "We thought we could help her control it, but we only stayed stuck and felt like failures."

All of us need to hear that Jesus Christ came to set us free from our addiction through his choice to bear our shame on the cross. Whether our addiction is sin or alcohol or something else, the solution is the same: We are freed only when we stop trying to free ourselves by our own willpower and simply relax in God's grace.

Recovering addicts use the slogan "Let go and let God." To help alcoholics, we must first let go and let God's grace break our addiction. Then we have something really helpful to offer alcoholic families.

Secret-Telling, Confidence-Keeping

In the same way the church hurts alcoholic families when it uses denial and shame, it also hurts them when it keeps secrets and breaks confidences. For the church to help the alcoholic family, it must learn the difference between a confidence and a secret. Keeping a confidence means honoring people's right to tell their own personal stories when, where, how and to whom they choose. Keeping a secret, on the other hand, involves withholding information that needs to be told to protect other people or the person sharing the information. See "Guidelines for Confidentiality" on page 100 for more details.

Ben finally found the courage to talk about his dad's alcoholism. It seemed best. His dad had entered an alcohol treatment center, and Ben needed someone to talk to about the unfamiliar changes in his family. He thought he could trust Chet, his youth minister.

After talking with Chet, Ben felt mixed emotions. He felt good that he had talked about the problem. Yet he feared he might not have done the right thing. The Alateen group he started attending affirmed his decision to break the "don't talk" rule. But in less than a week, his fear was confirmed.

After church the following Sunday, a woman Ben knew only by her saintly reputation approached him. Her words shocked him. "Ben," she said, "I was sorry to hear of your dad's drinking problem. But I'm glad he's getting help. I'm glad you and your family are receiving help as well. You can know we're praying for you."

Ben was stunned. It wasn't the words she spoke, but that she spoke them at all. He had talked with Chet in con-

Guidelines for Confidentiality

● As a general principle, don't share any part of a confidence with anyone. Period.

● If you learn about abuse, neglect, suicide threats, violence or threats of violence, take appropriate steps to intervene immediately. Contact community agencies that deal with these crises. Make it clear to the person who is giving you information that you cannot be bound by any pledge of confidence when a situation involves these secrets. Encourage the person to trust your judgment in such cases.

● Unless the person gives prior permission or specifically requests it, don't make the confidence a ''prayer concern''— not for staff or elders or on Sunday morning or in the bulletin or on the church prayer chain. Even if you don't give details, curiosity will drive people to snoop. It's better for them to know nothing than to know only enough to make them curious.

● If you feel it would help for someone else to know about the confidence, ask the person to share his or her story. If he or she says no, respect the response and don't push.

● Refuse to receive a secondhand confidence unless you know the person offering it has permission to share it.

● When you learn of confidences being shared inappropriately, confront the offender directly. Confront inappropriate secret-keeping as well.

fidence. How could she know? Who told her? What did she mean by "we're" praying for you? How many other people knew about his family's problem?

Feeling angry, hurt and betrayed, Ben went directly to Chet. Chet looked surprised at Ben's reaction. His explanation was painful to Ben. "I shared your situation as a prayer concern with our elders," he explained without hesitating. "And we put your family on the all-church prayer list. But we didn't mention the problem specifically." When Ben still looked confused, Chet added: "That's what we usually do. I thought you knew, so I didn't think there'd be a problem."

It was a problem to Ben. He left that Sunday embarrassed, hurt and angry. It was months before he returned. Even then, it was never the same.

Ben's experience is too common in the church. While we keep secrets to maintain an image, we betray confidences in our efforts to be helpful. And while secrets are harmful to alcoholic families, confidentiality is critical for at least two reasons:

● First, if the alcoholic is still drinking when the family learns that someone has broken the family secret, the "offender" could be at risk. I believe some form of abuse (physical, sexual, verbal, emotional or psychological) or neglect occurs in virtually all alcoholic families. Usually we learn about the abuse first. But when we learn about alcoholism while it is still occurring, we need to assume that some form of abuse is likely. Thus we can't risk any family member's safety or well-being by being loose-lipped.

● Second, if the alcoholic and family are recovering, a violation of confidentiality confirms the old unhealthy rules the family is trying to break: "don't talk," "don't trust," "don't feel."

One of the first things families learn in alcoholism recovery is to share their stories honestly with trustworthy people. When they open up only to learn later that we broke confidence, the voice of "don't trust" says to them: "See, that's just what I told you would happen if you talked. Now everyone knows. If only you'd kept your mouth shut like you learned. I was right, wasn't I?"

The church has proven that it can keep quiet about things. Each church I know has many secrets, but few have learned to keep confidences.

Smothering Love vs. Liberating Love

Many children of alcoholics feel victimized. They feel trapped and stripped of free will. Deep inside they may want someone to rescue them and take them far away from the pain.

Often the church is too willing to fulfill this desire. We smother the person with love, guidance and answers. But this approach rarely gives children of alcoholics the help they need for a healthy future. They need to learn that God has created them with a free will to make healthy choices for their lives. Instead of being smothered by nice gestures, children of alcoholics need to be liberated by a healthy love.

Everyone felt sorry for Lana. Her dad's alcoholism had already driven her mother away, and now it was threatening her dad's job. In an effort to help the struggling high schooler, kind church members offered Lana summer jobs, often hiring and keeping her on though she didn't have adequate skills. When she needed extra money during the school year, she'd frequently find an envelope stuffed with money in her purse. The only clue to its origin was written on the outside: A friend in Jesus.

When Lana graduated from high school, she decided not to go to college but to get a job. After all, she reasoned, she had always been able to get and keep a job with church members. Besides, a mysterious "friend in Jesus" was always there when she was most needy.

But her plans didn't materialize. No one hired her. Church members knew she was underskilled, and a full-time job was different from a summer job. Yet no one told her the truth. After months of discouraging and frustrating unemployment, Lana took the only job she could find—working for minimum wage at a fast-food restaurant.

Her church's smothering love—however well-intentioned—crippled Lana. For years she leaned on the church to help her. But only now has she begun to learn the responsibility and self-determination she needs to function as a healthy adult. She's 27.

The effects of smothering love—The smothering love the church often offers is a counterfeit of God's love. And its effects are lethal.

● Smothering love keeps people from facing the responsibility of their choices. This protection thwarts the growth that comes through making choices and living with consequences.

● Smothering love makes people conform and robs their free will. No matter how noble our intentions, when we make choices for people, we rob them of God's gift that makes them unique.

● Smothering love is, in reality, most unloving. If we truly love people, we give them the respect and dignity of making their own choices. Their choices may offend us. They may create even more pain and take them even further from God. But God's love demands that we allow them their own choices and still love them. Christ is our model. He loves us so much that he never interferes with our choices—even if they take us further from him.

● Smothering love and God's love have completely different boundaries. Smothering love has no limits. It will go anywhere, do anything, pay any price, sacrifice everything for the sake of the beloved. God's love, however, won't cross the frail boundary that separates his will from human will; it won't impose itself on us.

The possibilities of liberating love—Healing for alcoholic families is a difficult and often painful road. We can encourage, cheer and exhort. But we can't carry alcoholic families out of their problem. No matter how much we want to help, we must not rush in and take over where God himself will not.

More than once Jesus left people in their pain because they chose not to follow his healing way. When we work with children of alcoholics we too may be called upon to let them choose pain instead of recovery. But we must also remember that as Jesus never withdrew his love, we must not either.

Jesus Christ intends to liberate us. His hope is that we will choose to follow him. But he knows we may not. In his choice to liberate us, he offers us his incredible, unconditional love. "But God demonstrates his own love for us in this: While we were still sinners, Christ died for us" (Romans 5:8).

The actions I'm suggesting may seem unkind if we're used to being Nice (but ineffective) Helpers. It's easy to slip across that fragile line that separates Healthy Help from Nice Help. And sometimes it's hard to know a truly healthy response. Yet being a Healthy Helper is essential to creating a stable, healing place for children of alcoholics.

When the Church Helps

Only recently have I been in a church that is truly helpful to alcoholic families. It has no special program to reach victims of alcoholism. Yet more and more of them are coming into the fellowship. What's attracting these COAs to this church?

During my brief time in the church, I've identified several qualities of the fellowship that would be important to any family—whether alcoholic or not:

Unconditional love—Everyone is made to feel welcome in the church's services and meetings. No strings are attached.

Vulnerability—Members are affirmed in their humanity and willingness to risk sharing frankly about their struggles, regardless of their status or position in the church.

Confidentiality—The church treats the personal stories of its members as prized gifts not to be disregarded or passed on to others.

One congregation member—a child of two alcoholic parents—described his experience in the church to me. "I feel really loved and accepted here," he said. "They know me, and I know them. But we don't judge each other. I don't think I could ever do anything to lose the love of these people. You can't know how good it is to feel this way."

Is this a perfect church? No, not at all. Its pastor and members make no pretenses. But it does stand forth as a model of what can be done when the church truly helps.

Work It Out

1. How does your church respond to the "gut honesty" of its attenders?

2. Has your church had to face the presence of alcoholism in one of its families? If so, what happened?

3. Does your church have an "official" view of alcoholism or addiction? If so, what is it? Would your church's viewpoint tend to attract or repel alcoholics and their families?

4. What, if any, is the difference between "calling sin *sin*" and holding people responsible for their destructive behaviors?

5. How would you describe the kind of love your church gives to its hurting members? attenders? non-attenders within the community?

Endnotes

[1]*Alcoholics Anonymous* (New York: Alcoholics Anonymous World Services Inc., 1976), 44.

[2]M. Scott Peck, *People of the Lie: The Hope for Healing Human Evil* (New York: Simon & Schuster, 1983), 63.

[3]Peck, *People of the Lie: The Hope for Healing Human Evil*, 76.

[4]*Alcoholics Anonymous*, 13.

CHAPTER 7

Taking Off the Masks

Discovering the Need in the Youth Group

Reggie never took his eyes off my hand resting on his shoulder. What I thought was a gesture of affirmation, he regarded as a threat.

Sensing his fear, I slowly and carefully removed my hand.

Reggie relaxed.

I've known Reggie since he was in grade school, and we've always been friends. Yet my shoulder squeeze—usually appropriate with a youth group member—charged him with anxiety. He must have feared my hand would turn into a fist that would crash into his face. He had learned to expect that kind of abusive touch from a drunk father.

Reggie is from an alcoholic family. He's also a member of a church youth group. While he doesn't identify alcoholism as a problem in his family, he does admit that his dad sometimes drinks too much and "gets crazy." In truth, Reggie's dad is an active alcoholic whose health is being threatened by the addiction. Reggie's denial not only guards the family secret, it also keeps him from seeing how the alcoholism affects him.

When we learn of these "Reggies" in our youth groups, we begin wrestling with ways to help them. We struggle with difficult questions:

● Can the church really make a difference for these teenagers?

● How do we address a problem that is, by its nature, hidden?

Understanding Our Limits

As the body of Christ, the church can enable children of alcoholics to begin the healing process. However, we must be realistic. Several factors limit our effectiveness in reaching these young people:

Alcoholic families maintain an unhealthy balance. Left in their troubled families, children of alcoholics are people at risk. Yet they're also survivors. Most have learned ways to survive until they're old enough to get out. When we try to help teenagers in alcoholic families, we upset the families' rules that hide the problem. As a result, revealing the problem may actually increase the risk for these kids, especially in abusive families.

We have no guarantees. When we reach out to alcoholic families, we can't be sure they'll cooperate in the teenagers' healing. In fact, usually the opposite happens: Families regroup and work even harder to deny the alcoholism.

We may not reach the whole family. Sometimes it's most appropriate to help the teenager without getting directly involved in helping the whole family. Educator Charles Deutsch believes that children of alcoholics can begin healing whether or not the whole family is involved in the healing process. In *Broken Bottles, Broken Dreams: Understanding and Helping Children of Alcoholics*, he writes, "Help for the children need not and cannot be contingent upon treating the parents."[1]

Helping the teenager won't "save" the family.

Deutsch contends that children of alcoholics who understand alcoholism can become "potent catalysts for family recovery."[2] While this may be true, we must not use helping the teenager as a ploy for trying to save the family. Indeed, by using the teenager to "save" the family, we may actually be reinforcing the child's dysfunctional role as Family Hero.

We can't solve the problem. As Healthy Helpers, we must recognize we can't do for children of alcoholics—or their families—what they are not willing to do for themselves. We can't make them well. We can't fix them.

It takes time. We must accept that it take years for COAs or other family members to break the silence and begin recovery. One study found that, on average, it takes about seven years to move from the onset of alcoholism to the alcoholic's first contact with a treatment facility.[3] Though God is still in the miracle business, we ought not expect many overnight turnabouts when working with alcoholic families.

Knowing the limitations, we may be tempted merely to pray for these children and hope for the best. But the temptation doesn't last when we remember Jesus' words in Matthew 25:45: "I tell you the truth, whatever you did not do for one of the least of these, you did not do for me."

While we can't compel others to receive our help, Jesus' teachings certainly compel us to offer help. And—with the Holy Spirit's power—our help may indeed become a catalyst for healing.

Once we feel compelled to offer help, where do we begin? How do we offer help that's healthy? The process begins with the following two "Helping Gifts," which bring the problem out of hiding:

- Raising awareness
- Identifying the victims

Chapters 8 and 9 discuss five additional Helping Gifts.

Raising Awareness

In recent months, I've spoken at a couple of ministers

conferences and several churches about my concern for alcoholic families. Each time people have responded by saying they appreciate the information and are concerned about doing something in their church and community. Their response is encouraging—but even more so when someone actually does something with the information.

One minister returned to his congregation and shared the information in a series of Sunday morning messages. As a result, the church decided to sponsor a series of informational and training meetings for its members and the community.

A youth worker shared the information she received with her group. Within three weeks, two kids discussed their parents' alcoholism with her. The youth worker helped them find an Alateen group, and she's asked to use church facilities for new Alateen and Adult Children of Alcoholics support group meetings.

Finally, a young man left one conference personally distressed. Referring to the resource list I provided, he bought a couple of books. Within weeks, he admitted his dad's alcoholism, and he began meeting with other adult children of alcoholics in a support group. Today he's experiencing healing and hope.

These stories illustrate how sharing information is vital. As the church learns more, it will become aware of the presence of alcoholic families and sensitive to their needs. And only as young people learn about alcoholism will the children of alcoholics among them begin to face their families' problem.

An important step, then, in helping children of alcoholics in your youth group is to raise awareness. Study the subject periodically with your group. Topics to cover include:

- Alcohol's images, roles and use in our society
- Ways to handle the pressure to drink
- Alcohol's appropriate and inappropriate uses
- The difference between alcohol abuse and alcoholism
- Your church's beliefs about alcohol use

● The symptoms of alcoholism

● The effects of alcoholism on alcoholics and their families

● Resources to help with the alcohol problem

● The meaning of recovery—what needs to happen and how to support victims in the healing process

You won't be able to cover all this information in one session. Moreover, if you had to produce all this material yourself, you'd probably never have time. Fortunately numerous awareness materials are already available, including books, curricula and films. Here are some resources:

● On page 181 is a youth group meeting titled "When a Parent Drinks Too Much." It addresses the basic issues to include in an awareness meeting.

● Many of the best resources I've found on alcoholism and children of alcoholics are listed on page 197. These resources provide a solid foundation for a creative awareness program.

● An excellent resource is a nearby alcoholism treatment center. Consult your Yellow Pages under Alcoholism Information and Treatment. Many treatment centers provide speakers and programs.

● Ask a recovering adult child of an alcoholic to lead your group in a discussion of alcoholism's effect on the family. Recovering adult COAs have often done research (particularly if they're Family Heroes!), and their personal experiences add to the impact of the facts they share.

● One resource deserves special attention because of its unique appeal. The National Association for Children of Alcoholics (NACoA) has developed a poster series and a comic book to raise awareness among alcoholism's young victims. Well-known comic book characters give messages of help and hope to children of alcoholics on six different posters. Some of these:

The Amazing Spider-Man says: "If your mom or dad drinks too much, you're not alone. There are millions of kids with alcoholic parents."

The Incredible Hulk assures kids by saying:
"You can still love your mom and dad and get
help for yourself."
Simply hang these posters in your Sunday school rooms
or youth room. They may prompt young people to come to
you with their questions because they see that you understand their situation. (See resource listing on page 197 for
NACoA's address.)

Identifying the Victims

How do you identify a particular teenager as the child
of an alcoholic? The best way is for a young person to approach you after recognizing the same dynamics at home
that you talk about in an awareness program. This happens
often. I have yet to speak to a group about alcoholic families without having at least one person identify himself or
herself as a COA.

But it isn't always this simple.

Children of alcoholics don't see identification as helpful. Rather, identification means they've been discovered.
Someone else knows the family secret. They'll be anxious
and uneasy when they learn that you know.

When children of alcoholics don't come to you with
their problem, identifying them in your youth group usually
begins with your gut feeling that something's not quite
right. Any time you have this suspicion, it's worth investigating. But please do it appropriately.

It's not ethical—or helpful—to check your suspicion by
approaching the teenager's friends or extended family. This
approach is dangerously close to gossiping, and it can back-
fire. If the teenager learns you are playing private eye, he or
she may get scared off or decide you're untrustworthy.

Don't sneak around trying to learn the truth. Instead,
spend time getting to know the teenager better and learning
what you can about the family firsthand. If your suspicion is
wrong, both you and the teenager benefit from a stronger
personal relationship.

Sometimes our suspicions are wrong—in whole or in part. For example, I strongly suspected Terry was living with an alcoholic parent but was in deep denial about his troubled family. As I got better acquainted, I learned my guess was way off base.

I was right that some stress in Terry's family was making him "act out" in a way similar to children from alcoholic families. In truth, though, his brother was dying of AIDS. Because of the disease's social stigma, the family had chosen to suffer together in silence ("don't talk").

Terry did need help. However, if I hadn't taken the time to check the situation, I wouldn't have helped him at all. Since I got to know Terry better, I could correctly identify the problem and help him find appropriate assistance.

As you spend time with a teenager who may be the child of an alcoholic, test your suspicion by keeping your eyes, ears and feelings alert for the following clues. Use the questions to guide your thinking. (Another option is to give Dr. John W. Jones' Children of Alcoholics Screening Test on page 114 to youth group members you suspect may be from alcoholic families.)

Clue #1: Family rules—The first clue to an alcoholic or otherwise dysfunctional family involves the family rules outlined in Chapter 3. Does the teenager seem to follow the "don't talk," "don't trust" and "don't feel" rules?

● Does the young person have trouble talking easily and freely?

● Does the teenager have difficulty identifying and verbalizing basic emotions besides anger?

● Does he or she resist inviting you home?

● If and when you've visited the home, does the family seem to be hiding something?

● Does the family appear not to give all family members unconditional love, acceptance, affirmation and nurturing?

● Do the family's actions seem more like a performance for your benefit than genuine interaction?

● Do you sense that the teenager "walks on eggshells"

Children of Alcoholics Screening Test

Check the box that best fits your experience. If you're unsure of how to answer a question, leave it blank.

1. Have you ever thought that one of your parents had a drinking problem?   Yes ☑   No ☐

2. Have you ever lost sleep because of a parent's drinking?   Yes ☑   No ☐

3. Did you ever encourage one of your parents to quit drinking?   Yes ☐   No ☑

4. Did you ever feel alone, scared, nervous, angry, or frustrated because a parent was not able to stop drinking?   Yes ☐   No ☐

5. Did you ever argue or fight with a parent when he or she was drinking?   Yes ☐   No ☑

6. Did you ever threaten to run away from home because of a parent's drinking?   Yes ☐   No ☑

7. Has a parent ever yelled at or hit you or other family members when drinking?   Yes ☑   No ☐

8. Have you ever heard your parents fight when one of them was drunk?   Yes ☑   No ☐

9. Did you ever protect another family member from a parent who was drinking?   Yes ☑   No ☐

10. Did you ever feel like hiding or emptying a parent's bottle of liquor?   Yes ☑   No ☐

11. Do many of your thoughts revolve around a problem drinking parent or difficulties that arise because of his or her drinking?   Yes ☐   No ☐

12. Did you ever wish that a parent would stop drinking?   Yes ☑   No ☐

13. Did you ever feel responsible for and guilty about a parent's drinking?   Yes ☐   No ☑

14. Did you ever fear that your parents would get divorced due to alcohol misuse?   Yes ☐   No ☑

15. Have you ever withdrawn from and avoided outside activities and friends because of embarrassment and shame over a parent's drinking problem?   Yes ☐   No ☑

16. Did you ever feel caught in the middle of an argument or fight between a problem drinking parent and your other parent?   Yes ☐   No ☑

continued

17. Did you ever feel that you made a parent drink alcohol?   Yes ☐   No ☑

18. Have you ever felt that a problem drinking parent did not really love you?   Yes ☐   No ☑

19. Did you ever resent a parent's drinking?   Yes ☑   No ☐

20. Have you ever worried about a parent's health because of his or her alcohol use?   Yes ☐   No ☑

21. Have you ever been blamed for a parent's drinking?   Yes ☐   No ☑

22. Did you ever think your father was an alcoholic?   Yes ☐   No ☑

23. Did you ever wish your home could be more like the homes of your friends who did not have a parent with a drinking problem?   Yes ☑   No ☐

24. Did a parent ever make promises to you that he or she did not keep because of drinking?   Yes ☐   No ☐

25. Did you ever think your mother was an alcoholic?   Yes ☐   No ☐

26. Did you ever wish that you could talk to someone who could understand and help the alcohol-related problems in your family?   Yes ☐   No ☐

27. Did you ever fight with your brothers and sisters about a parent's drinking?   Yes ☐   No ☑

28. Did you ever stay away from home to avoid the drinking parent or your other parent's reaction to the drinking?   Yes ☑   No ☐

29. Have you ever felt sick, cried, or had a "knot" in your stomach after worrying about a parent's drinking?   Yes ☑   No ☐

30. Did you ever take over any chores and duties at home that were usually done by a parent before he or she developed a drinking problem?   Yes ☐   No ☐

Count your total number of "yes" responses. If that number is six or more, you can assume you're the child of an alcoholic parent. Talk about your answers to this survey with a qualified counselor.

Children of Alcoholics Screening Test © 1983 by Dr. John W. Jones, PhD. Used by permission of Camelot Unlimited, 5 N. Wabash, Ste. 1409, Dept. 18GBK, Chicago, IL 60602. Telephone: (312) 938-8861. All rights reserved. Contact the publisher for copies of *The Children of Alcoholics Screening Test and Test Manual*, which includes multiple copies of the test as well as a test manual with detailed information on the test's reliability, relevant case studies, and instructions for administering, scoring and interpreting C.A.S.T.

at home?

These questions hint at whether the teenager's home environment is healthy or unhealthy. "Yes" answers may reveal the presence of the three rules of alcoholic families.

Clue #2: Roles and behavior—Does the young person seem to fit one or two of the family roles described in Chapter 4? As you consider these questions, keep in mind that it's easiest to identify the Scapegoat by behavior. The others (Family Hero, Mascot and Lost Child) tend to blend into the crowd.

● Does the teenager have difficulty concentrating?

● Is the teenager always extremely busy?

● Does he or she exhibit a hair-trigger temper or other signs of emotional fragility?

● Does the young person seek to keep peace by carefully avoiding disagreements or conflicts?

● Is the teenager frequently late, especially to early church services or activities?

● Is he or she frequently absent, especially from Saturday night and Sunday morning events?

● Does the young person's behavior seem too immature or mature for the teenager's age or developmental stage?

● Does the teenager have poor personal hygiene?

● Does the young person dress inappropriately for current weather conditions?

● Does he or she express excessive concern to get right home after meetings and events?

● Does the teenager frequently act and look tired?

● Does the young person always find excuses for not hosting a meeting or entertaining friends at home?

● Does he or she seek your approval by being a "good Christian" and always doing what you say is right?

● Does the teenager have difficulty making and keeping friends?

● Has the teenager's delinquent behavior resulted in trouble with school, legal or church authorities?

● Does the teenager frequently complain about physical problems, especially headaches or stomachaches?

- Is the teenager a bully?
- Is the young person extremely withdrawn—a chronic wallflower?

"Yes" answers to different questions indicate the different roles a teenager in an alcoholic family may have adopted in order to survive.

Clue #3: Reaction to holidays—There's no more difficult season for the child of an alcoholic than from Thanksgiving through New Year's Day. A holiday from work isn't a holiday for the family of an alcoholic. A day off almost always means drinking, which always results in heightened family friction.

- Does the young person anticipate holidays with anxiety, sullenness and fear?
- Is the teenager reluctant to talk about family holiday plans?
- Does he or she withdraw when the conversation turns to "what our family did for the holidays?"
- Does the teenager exaggerate holiday plans, revealing that he or she obviously has created a fantasy world?

Religious holidays can be especially tough for children of alcoholics, because these holidays are supposed to be filled with joy. It seems the greater the anticipation attached to a holiday, the heavier the dread and anxiety COAs feel. If a teenager becomes extremely anxious around holidays that are usually festive, something may be wrong at home.

Clue #4: Fantasy life—In order to survive, children of alcoholics create their own fantasy world. It shapes the way they each look at their family and life.

- Does the teenager's description of family life seem more positive than your personal knowledge and experience of the family indicate?
- Do you sense the young person is telling you how he or she would like things to be at home rather than how things really are?

Coping in an alcoholic family often means creating a dream world because the real world is too difficult. If a teenager lives in a fantasy, find out what's wrong with the real world.

Clue #5: Reports of abuse—Since the correlation between addiction and family violence is strong, reports of abuse suggest the possibility of alcoholism. When kids report family violence to me, I look for the circumstances behind the abuse. I nearly always find alcoholism or some other addiction in the family.

● Does the family have a history of any form of abuse?

● Has the child reported physical, emotional or sexual abuse to you or anyone else?

● Have you suspected this youth group member is a victim of family violence?

● Does the teenager either flinch from physical touch or seem "skin hungry"—clinging inappropriately to other people?

We usually see evidence of family violence before we learn of a drinking problem. If questions of abuse arise with a teenager, check into the possibility that alcoholism may be the real cause.

Clue #6: Extreme attitude toward alcohol use—Youth workers are barraged with information about teenage alcohol abuse. We now know that about 3 million teenagers are alcoholic.[4]

Many church youth workers attribute teenage alcohol abuse to negative peer influence. I don't disagree with this conclusion. But I think there's a more common, substantial reason: Many teenagers may abuse alcohol because they've learned that lifestyle from their parents.

● Does the teenager frequently use or abuse alcohol?

● Does the young person have extreme views of alcohol—either glamorizing alcohol use or becoming a vocal, strident opponent of any alcohol use?

● During discussions of alcoholism and its effects on families, does the teenager's behavior change significantly?

Alcohol abuse or a reactionary response against alcohol can indicate a misuse of alcohol at home. Either extreme merits further investigation.

Clue #7: Unusual struggle with spirituality and

self-esteem—A fundamental problem for children of alcoholics is low self-esteem. Their parents don't offer the needed nurture and support during childhood and adolescence. As a result, these children live with deep-seated questions about their own worth and their relationship to God.

• Does the teenager seem to struggle to develop a positive self-esteem?

• Does the young person have difficulty believing God really loves him or her?

• Does the teenager have trouble relating to God as a loving parent?

• Does the teenager have difficulty feeling forgiven by God, other people, or himself or herself?

• Does the young person seem to follow God more out of fear than love?

Low self-esteem can point to many different problems—some of which may grow out of the teenager's own behavior and choices. But many times, low self-esteem ultimately indicates deeper problems with families and parents. Thus, it's important to investigate the reasons behind the low self-esteem. Alcoholism at home may be a factor.

Interpreting the Clues

These questions can help you decide whether your suspicion of family alcoholism is correct. Numerous "yes" answers may indicate a problem. But as you apply these clues to those you think may be victims, be careful how you interpret and use the answers. Use the following guidelines:

• Look for a pattern to the responses. A few scattered clues may indicate a problem in the family. But the problem might not be alcoholism.

• Remember that all families live on a continuum from more healthy to less healthy. Each will exhibit dysfunctional behaviors from time to time regardless of its overall health. Family rules, survival roles and low self-esteem emerge in various dysfunctional behaviors. However, the rules pertaining to reactions to holidays, abuse and violence, and attitudes toward alcohol use correlate much more specifically with parental alcoholism. Thus, clues #1, #2, #4 and #7 need to be evaluated in light of clues #3, #5 and #6.

● Look for temporary stresses and tensions within the family that may be upsetting an otherwise healthy situation, but from which the family will recover once the stress passes. These include severe illnesses, job changes, moving, major surgery, death in the family, school adjustments and lifestyle changes.

● Get to know a recovering adult child of an alcoholic whose firsthand insights and stories can help you understand and recognize patterns in group members from alcoholic families.

● Before you leap to action, always check your assessment with a professional who is trained to identify and help victims of alcoholism. This book can't give you professional-level understanding and expertise. Rather, it guides you toward higher awareness and a basic understanding of the complex issues facing victims of alcoholism.

While all these clues are important, they shouldn't be used as an excuse to pass judgment from a distance. They can't reflect *all* the dynamics that may be present in a teenager's family. Therefore, it's important to build trusting, healthy friendships with teenagers who may be from alcoholic families but aren't willing to break the family secret. Through your friendship, the young person may risk talking to you. That self-revelation opens the door for you to offer the next Helping Gift: intervention.

Work It Out

1. Do you agree that the church can play a vital role in healing teenagers from alcoholic families? Why or why not? What would you say are gifts the church has to offer these families?

2. Of the limiting factors listed on page 108, which do you see as the greatest obstacle for your ministry to teenagers from alcoholic families? Pray that God will help you overcome that obstacle.

3. How well do you think your church and youth group members understand alcoholism and its effects on the family? Think of specific ways to raise awareness in your congregation.

4. List the people and resources that might be useful for an alcohol awareness program. Include books, videos, local counselors and adult children of alcoholics. How does the list's length surprise you?

Endnotes

[1]Charles Deutsch, *Broken Bottles, Broken Dreams: Understanding and Helping Children of Alcoholics* (New York: Teachers College Press, 1982), Preface.

[2]Deutsch, *Broken Bottles, Broken Dreams: Understanding and Helping Children of Alcoholics*, Preface.

[3]Cited in Conrad Bergendoff, *Pastoral Care for Alcoholism: An Introduction* (Center City, MN: Hazelden Educational Materials, 1981), 9.

[4]Eugene C. Roehlkepartain (editor), *The Youth Ministry Resource Book* (Loveland, CO: Group Books, 1988), 132.

CHAPTER 8

Moving Toward Healing

Creating a Safe Place for COAs in the Youth Group

Whenever we learn that a particular family may be alcoholic, our first reaction may be denial. We say to ourselves: I know that family. Sure, the parents may have a drink every once in a while. But they couldn't be alcoholic. This kid must be trying to get back at Mom and Dad for something.

Such a response may seem natural, but it isn't healthy. It's important to trust a teenager's story instead of our own perception of the family. Too often we give greater weight to what we *think* we know than to what a teenager says.

Instead, we need to listen to, accept and believe a teenager's story about alcohol abuse at home—until we're thoroughly convinced otherwise. The accusation is so serious that it indicates one of two things:

1. The teenager is telling the truth. This is usually the case. Teenagers from alcoholic families won't flippantly break their families' rules and roles. In fact, kids who tell about an alcohol problem at home often feel they've betrayed their family. They may even feel their lives are threatened.

2. If the teenager tries to con you into believing alcoholism is a problem at home, something else is wrong with the parent-teenager relationship. In this case, investigating the situation will likely uncover the real needs and open the door to other important ministry.

When you believe a youth group member is from an alcoholic family, you can offer Healthy Help through several Helping Gifts. There's no specific order for giving these gifts, and they don't make up a pat formula for rescuing the victims of alcoholism. But each is an important part of healing the wounds of a COA. This chapter deals with four Helping Gifts that follow the gifts of awareness and identification in Chapter 7: intervention, referral, support and a healthy family model. Chapter 9 focuses on a final gift: hope.

Intervention

On their own, alcoholics rarely seek help before they "hit bottom"—when they reach a point where they have no choice but to seek help. If left alone, most alcoholics would drink until they lost their families, jobs and health. And some would never hit bottom—until they hit the bottom of a grave.

The same pattern holds true for other victims of alcoholism, such as the spouse and children. While all are in painful situations, none will seek help until the discomfort becomes intolerable.

Despite this reality, we don't need to wait for victims of alcoholism to hit bottom and come to us for help. Giving Healthy Help requires that we intervene. As Conrad Bergendoff writes, "One does not 'help' an alcoholic; one thrusts reality upon him or her."[1] And we thrust reality upon the victims of alcoholism by allowing situations or circumstances in which they must personally face the consequences of the addiction. In the process, they hit bottom a little quicker. Then we give them firm, direct counsel to accept professional help.

Intervention is one of the most difficult Helping Gifts to offer a child of an alcoholic. And it's the most difficult gift for that child to accept. That's because it involves pain. We don't like increasing the young person's discomfort, and the young person doesn't like feeling it. Thus we may be tempted to be Nice Helpers. However, until we accept that pain plays a role in helping alcoholic families, we won't ever give the gift of intervention.

Brad is a youth worker who is sensitive to the unique needs of kids from alcoholic families. As a result, he has successfully helped several COAs. Yet he's haunted by the memory of one teenage girl he couldn't help.

Rhoda had been attending Brad's church for about six months before she got involved in the youth group. When she did get involved, she became very active, and Brad built a friendship with her.

Then Brad began to notice the warning signs that usually point to parental alcoholism. Rhoda quickly declined whenever he suggested someone from the church drop by to talk with her parents. In a meeting that focused on alcoholism, he noticed that Rhoda's mood changed from intense to disinterested to depressed. He noticed she talked about lots of responsibility at home; she did laundry, frequently cooked and almost always shopped for the family. Finally, Rhoda seemed to have trouble just having fun—she seemed too responsible, too grown up for a 16-year-old.

All in all, something just didn't seem right in Rhoda's life. Finally, Brad decided to talk to Rhoda to learn more and to find out if his suspicion was correct.

Rhoda unconvincingly denied that either of her parents had an alcohol problem. Brad reminded her that God wanted her to have a full, happy life. Further, he assured her he wanted to help her face anything that was keeping her from realizing God's best for her. Finally, Brad thanked her for talking to him and assured her he was willing to talk more any time.

Though Brad felt disappointed he hadn't made more

progress, he felt good that he had at least brought the subject into the open. He was confident Rhoda would eventually request additional help.

But that was the last time he saw Rhoda. When she didn't attend church or youth group the next two Sundays, Brad called her at home. Rhoda was unavailable. Her mother took his number and promised to have Rhoda return the call.

Brad never received a call from Rhoda. But he did get a letter. Rhoda thanked Brad for his call and informed him she would no longer be attending his church or youth group. Her folks, she said, wanted her to attend another church.

Rhoda's letter confirmed what Brad had hoped to learn, but it was too late. Through the experience, Brad learned a valuable truth about helping COAs: While they may be drawn to church by an unconscious desire for help, they really don't want help that is healthy. They want to be helped on their own terms—without the healing pain of discovery. In short, they prefer the Nice Help we usually prefer to give.

A therapist and friend gave me a wall hanging that has helped me understand the healing role of pain. Its message: "Your pain is the breaking of the shell that encloses your understanding." The alcoholic family has enclosed itself within a shell of deception and denial to avoid seeing its problem with understanding. It will be painful when that shell cracks and begins to break away. But unless the shell cracks, no healing can occur.

The pain of intervention is a good, healing pain. It seeks to bring the victims of alcoholism to where they must make a tough choice: receive help or remain victims. Either choice has consequences. The first will mean increased discomfort for a time. But it holds the promise of health and happiness. The second choice means continuing current patterns until the numbing pain of victimization becomes greater than the fear of receiving help.

A difficult dilemma—practical and ethical—faces us when we work with children of alcoholics living in violent families. While intervention may provide help, it may also increase the young person's risk. In such situations, the youth worker faces two difficult options:

1. Intervene now, knowing the young person's desire for wellness and healing may actually increase the risk of retribution from other family members who don't want the secret out.

2. Leave the young person alone to survive the best he or she can. Intervene after the young person leaves home; hope he or she will be safe in the meantime.

I know few adult children of alcoholics who, as children or teenagers, didn't yearn for the Helping Gift of intervention. Even with its risks, most feel it would have been better than the hell they endured.

Intervention can refer to many different procedures that, hopefully, have the same outcome. We'll look at two common strategies. One is a crisis intervention in response to an immediate, critical need. The other is a process that moves victims—when there's no immediate threat or danger—toward help over a longer period of time.

Crisis intervention—Crisis intervention requires specialized training and is best done by or with professionals. Thus most youth workers won't use it themselves. If you feel a teenager needs this type of intervention because the teenager is in immediate danger at home (such as physical or sexual abuse), seek assistance from local resources:

● Many school systems have trained intervention teams of teachers, coaches and counselors. Find out if your school system has such teams and become familiar with their procedures.

● Employee Assistance Programs, which are offered by alcoholism treatment centers and many workplaces, can provide leadership and guidance for such intervention.

A youth worker's role in crisis intervention focuses primarily on referring the teenager to professional help, which is discussed on page 130.

Long-term intervention—Youth workers will be most effective with children of alcoholics when they approach intervention as a process. Here are some things you can do as a Healthy Helper:

● Take care of yourself before and as you help others. Make sure you maintain your emotional health and relate to others in trust, honesty and openness.

● Immediately report evidence of suspected child abuse to the appropriate authorities.

In my state, church workers aren't required by law to report to authorities information they learn in the confidentiality of a counseling or confessional setting. As a result, some pastors and youth workers don't report obvious signs of neglect or physical, mental or sexual abuse.

Ministers don't report abuse for several reasons. Sometimes they fear the congregation won't support them. They know how uncomfortable it is to stand alone, and they're not willing to risk it.

A more common reason for not reporting abuse, however, is that ministers rationalize it away. They can't believe such a thing could happen, because their church forbids or teaches against the behavior. Or the sources seem unreliable. Maybe they "just can't believe the mother would do that." Or they confront the perpetrators by asking if the accusations are true, receive a "no" answer and simply drop the matter. I've even known of confronted perpetrators who confessed to abuse, but because they promised to never do it again, the ministers didn't report the problems to authorities.

Each of these responses is irresponsible. They may seem the easiest because they don't cause pain, but such attitudes epitomize Nice Help at its worst. And they endanger the health and even the lives of the children who are victims of the abuse.

● Get acquainted with people in your community who provide treatment and counseling to alcoholic families. Develop a referral list and share it with other church workers.

● Work with your church staff and local alcoholism professionals to develop a strategy for helping victims of alcoholism who attend your church. Use the resources these organizations offer, and invite the leaders to learn about your church and its outreach to alcoholics and their families.

● Spend time getting to know each youth group member. Watch for telltale signs of family alcoholism described in Chapter 7.

● Regularly assure your group that you and your staff are trustworthy people. Let kids know you can hear anything they have to say without judgment. Verbalize your concern for each teenager, and assure the group that you respect confidences.

● When you suspect family alcoholism, don't hesitate to confront the issue. However, don't *accuse* someone in the teenager's family of being alcoholic. Young people will invariably deny that a parent is an alcoholic. Instead, simply ask the young person if anyone in the family drinks too much. If the teenager denies it, don't be surprised or discouraged. Your suspicion may still be true. By bringing up the subject, you give the young person permission to talk about it later.

Honestly and lovingly confronting alcoholic families about their problem is an essential element of Healthy Help. This confrontation may take many forms. Confrontation can be as simple as a referral to an agency. Or it may be as difficult as breaking confidence in order to tell the "secret" to those who can bring help. A face-to-face meeting is often not particularly helpful because of the denial in which alcoholic families live.

● Detach with love, and don't nag. Once you've told a young person what you know, shared your concerns and presented some options, let the teenager decide what happens next. Don't rescue him or her by saying what to do. The person's pain may intensify at this point, but that's necessary for healing to take place.

● Once you've shared your concern, don't forget about the person. Let him or her know you'll be there with appropriate help. Assure the young person of your continued help and support through the healing process.

● When a child of an alcoholic expresses a desire for help, be prepared to assist and support by referring the young person to an alcoholism treatment center, a counselor and/or a 12-Step support group. This referral is another Helping Gift in itself.

Referral

Children of alcoholics face numerous and complex issues—abandonment, loss of a normal childhood, incest, grief, divorce, abuse or suicidal thoughts. As a result, healing and recovery often take a long time and require expert counseling.

Few youth workers or pastors have time for such an extended counseling ministry. And even fewer possess adequate training and experience to counsel children of alcoholics or their families. Until more church workers receive training, I believe we need to look beyond the church to people who can help the COAs we know.

This is not to say that youth workers can't help children of alcoholics. Quite the opposite: Recovering children of alcoholics need many people in their healing process. Though you may not be the best person to function as therapist or counselor, you may be the best—and, in some cases, the only—source of support. This is an invaluable role for youth workers and churches.

I recommend always referring children of alcoholics to professionals for assessment and treatment. And to ensure I don't smother teenagers with my help, I ask them to make the first contact. This tests their sincerity and gives them the gift of responsibility.

Competent referral begins with a referral list. To build your list, contact a local mental health or social service agency, or a hospital with alcoholism treatment services. Specifically ask for the names of counselors to whom they refer children of alcoholics. While there are numerous professionals working with alcoholics and their spouses, the number working with COAs is still small since the specialty is new. However, with some digging, you should be able to find qualified professionals.

Soon after intervention, refer the COA to a counselor

who can conduct a thorough assessment. Assessment is critical for several reasons:

● It will confirm your suspicions concerning the alcoholism's effects on the child.

● The counselor can determine the extent and severity of the teenager's problem.

● A professional can recommend the most appropriate help for a particular situation and young person. See "Services for COAs" on page 132 for information on the options.

Selection of qualified counselors—Now the question is: What attributes do we look for to make a competent referral? Professionals who specialize in counseling and treating children of alcoholics usually work in (or in close association with) alcoholism treatment centers or agencies. A few are in private counseling practices. To locate them:

● Look in your Yellow Pages under Alcoholism Information and Treatment.

● Contact the local office of the National Council on Alcoholism. These offices can be extremely helpful in recommending—even providing—a professional to conduct the assessment.

● Check with Alcoholics Anonymous, Al-Anon and Adult Children of Alcoholics organizations and treatment centers.

I generally don't recommend seeking professional assessment and treatment for COAs from psychologists, doctors, psychiatrists, general-practice counselors or Christian counselors, unless they've had specialized training or extensive experience in the area (which is still rare).

When I look for a professional to provide assessment and treatment, I look for four attributes. As you begin working more frequently with COAs in your church, you'll develop your own criteria.

1. Proven experience with alcoholic families—I never refer a COA to a counselor who doesn't have proven competence in this field. This only makes good sense. If I personally can't vouch for a counselor's competence, I seek recommendations among people I know and trust. This is

Services for COAs

Several services are available to children of alcoholics and their families. Here are options a counselor may recommend after assessment:

Individual counseling—While usually not as effective for addicts, it can be quite helpful for other victims of alcoholism. This is especially true if the COA needs to work on deeply personal issues, such as grief, abuse and self-esteem. However, individual counseling is usually best when coupled with support-group involvement.

12-Step support groups—Encourage any teenage COA to participate in Alateen or Al-Anon as a part of the healing and recovery program. These groups utilize the theory and recovery steps developed by Alcoholics Anonymous. Some COAs find regular attendance in these groups is enough to facilitate healing.

Group therapy—Group therapy isn't the same as a 12-Step or other support group. It's facilitated by a professional counselor who uses special techniques to encourage individuals—with the help of the group—to work through personal issues. Group therapy can be particularly helpful for COAs because, as they heal, they establish new rules and roles in relation to people other than the therapist.

Inpatient/outpatient treatment—Many treatment centers offer both inpatient and outpatient services. For inpatient treatment, a client moves into the center—usually for three to four weeks—for intense treatment. Participants have a rigorous daily schedule of reading, group therapy, 12-Step meetings and personal counseling.

Outpatient treatment involves a client living at home and coming to the center for treatment. Usually the client goes for treatment four or five evenings each week over a five- to six-week period—or longer. Another outpatient model is day treatment, in which the client spends each day (up to eight hours) at the center. Outpatient treatment includes the same elements as inpatient treatment, but it's usually less intense because of the limited time with treatment staff.

Group homes—A COA teenager may need to be placed in a group home if the family situation is severe or if the teenager's "acting out" behavior is creating problems. With the increasing awareness of the role alcoholism plays in troubled families, more group homes are addressing issues facing COAs. Group homes receive clients for several months—sometimes years. They may also help place teenagers in foster homes if necessary.

where my referral file really pays off. As I develop this list, I make contacts I am confident give me trustworthy information when the need arises.

2. *Understanding of alcoholism and the addictive family system*—By "understanding" I mean not only knowledge but also experience. When possible, I try to refer COAs to counselors who've experienced the effects of alcoholism as a COA, a spouse of an alcoholic or even a recovering alcoholic.

3. *Recovery from the effects of alcoholism*—It's one thing to be a victim of alcoholism. It's altogether different to be a recovering victim. If I send a COA to a professional who's a victim of alcoholism but has not experienced any personal healing, my efforts will be futile. The counselor's work would be severely hindered by his or her open wounds.

4. *Acceptance of 12-Step theory and programs*—Because I refer COAs to counselors who are often themselves recovering COAs, I choose counselors who participate in a 12-Step group and are "program people"—people who follow the basic 12-Step approach. To me, this involvement demonstrates their highest confidence in 12-Step support groups, and it assures me that the COA will be directed into a proven program of healing and recovery.

Having a program person as a counselor also assures me that his or her approach will be sympathetic to—if not in agreement with—basic Christian principles, because the 12-Step approach is rooted in Christian teachings. For more about this approach, see "Understanding the 12 Steps" on page 134.

My emphasis on the 12-Step approach disqualifies many Christian counselors. Frequently they reject the 12 Steps because they're uncomfortable with the steps' language, which isn't specifically Christian. Instead, they advocate other approaches that they say are more Christian. However, while their approaches may be valid, I'm reluctant to refer to them until they develop a proven track record.

The "Quizzing the Counselor" box on page 137 lists

Understanding the 12 Steps

Throughout the book I've referred to 12-Step groups such as Alcoholics Anonymous, Al-Anon, Alateen, and Adult Children of Alcoholics. These groups have an excellent record for helping victims of alcoholism.

These groups center around a 12-Step plan of recovery. The steps are also used effectively to help co-dependents and children of alcoholics find a new sense of serenity in their lives—by emphasizing acceptance, self-care, forgiveness, confession and trust in God.

The 12 Steps are compatible with scripture. In fact, they are based on scriptural principles identified by an Episcopal minister, Dr. Samuel Shoemaker, who developed a ministry to alcoholics during the 1930s in New York City. In 1934 an alcoholic businessman named Bill Wilson attended Shoemaker's group, known as the Oxford Group. During his detoxification effort, Wilson became deeply depressed. In the midst of this depression he experienced an amazing conversion-like experience.

Wilson later left the Oxford Group and put together a collection of writings that outlined his theories about alcoholism. He called his book *Alcoholics Anonymous*. It included the 12 Steps, which alcoholics and other addicts learn to follow through their support groups.

The 12 Steps of AA outline a plan of recovery for alcoholics, and have been adapted—with permission—for programs dealing with drug addicts, overeaters and addicts of other compulsive behaviors. The steps:

1. We admitted we were powerless over alcohol—that our lives had become unmanageable.

2. Came to believe that a Power greater than ourselves could restore us to sanity.

3. Made a decision to turn our will and our lives over to the care of God, *as we understood Him.*

continued

4. Made a searching and fearless moral inventory of ourselves.

5. Admitted to God, to ourselves, and to another human being, the exact nature of our wrongs.

6. Were entirely ready to have God remove all these defects of character.

7. Humbly asked Him to remove our shortcomings.

8. Made a list of all persons we had harmed, and became willing to make amends to them all.

9. Made direct amends to such people wherever possible, except when to do so would injure them or others.

10. Continued to take personal inventory and when we were wrong promptly admitted it.

11. Sought through prayer and meditation to improve our conscious contact with God *as we understood Him*, praying only for knowledge of His will for us and the power to carry that out.

12. Having had a spiritual awakening as the result of these steps, we tried to carry this message to alcoholics, and to practice these principles in all our affairs.

I confidently recommend the 12-Step approach as an effective tool for providing Healthy Help to your teenagers. To be clear, I'm not recommending that you lay aside the scriptures in favor of the 12 Steps. Rather, I believe the 12 Steps can complement the scriptures by providing a simple tool to use as you provide Healthy Help.

several questions to ask potential counselors before adding them to your referral list.

A valuable resource for more information about referrals is Will Maloney's *Chemical Dependency Treatment Programs: A Guide to Referral.*[2] It defines many terms used in alcoholism and chemical dependency treatment, explains the various services, and gives practical advice on making well-informed referrals.

Importance of patience—Referrals can be frustrating. Sometimes people don't follow through and make a recommended appointment. Sometimes your resource—no matter how well you've checked it out—isn't as good as you thought. And sometimes, for any number of unknown reasons, your referral just doesn't work. That's why it's always gratifying when a referral works.

Roseanne is one teenager who began healing because of a referral I made. Our first conversation followed a youth group meeting in which I shared my own story. She approached me to talk about her mom's alcoholism. Over the next number of months we had other conversations. Roseanne had trouble believing things were all that bad in her family, and she couldn't see that the situation was really hurting her.

Several times I encouraged Roseanne to contact a counselor I knew who could help her. But Roseanne always hesitated. She didn't have time. She didn't have money for the initial fee. She didn't think it would help. Each time, I simply told her to let me know when she was ready to make an appointment.

Finally, 15 months after our first talk, Roseanne called me to say she had made an appointment and had talked with the counselor. "I wish I'd talked with her sooner," she told me, "but I guess better now than never. I just want to thank you for encouraging me to call her. I'm going to start therapy in a new group she's forming next month."

Though it took Roseanne 15 months finally to do what she needed to do, it has paid off. Today she is active in COA support groups and is continuing to grow and heal.

Quizzing the Counselor

Here are eight questions to ask a counselor before adding him or her to your referral list. I've included what I want to hear (or not to hear) after each question. I don't expect you to agree with how I want each question answered. But I believe it's vital that you know at least how you want them answered before you ask. Most importantly, these are all appropriate questions. If anyone says he or she is unwilling or unable to answer a question, that person doesn't go on my referral list.

1. What do you believe about the basic nature of people?

I make referrals to counselors who see their clients as made in the image of God and as individuals who have the ability to make choices about their lives.

2. As a therapist, which role do you tend to assume most often with a client: an advice-giver, teacher, friend or con-fronter?

I avoid advice-givers, choosing counselors who comfortably use the other roles.

3. If a client you're working with fails to get better, whose fault is it?

I prefer counselors who say, "the client's." This doesn't mean the counselor blames the client, but that he or she sees the client as a person with freedom, power and responsibility.

4. What role does the client's family play in the client's development as a healthy or unhealthy person?

When counselors indicate they see the client's health connected to and reflecting the family's health, I'm satisfied.

5. Why do you think alcoholics are alcoholics?

With this question, I'm more concerned about what I don't want to hear: descriptions that blame, condemn and judge the alcoholic.

6. What is your experience with alcoholic families?

I prefer counselors who are recovering children of alcoholics and have experience working with these families in successful programs.

7. What experience do you have with support groups and treatment programs based on the 12-Steps of Alcoholics Anonymous?

I'm looking for a general affirmation of these programs.

8. What is your professional training?

I don't believe professional training is as important as experience in working with alcoholic families. However, I prefer to refer to people who have training in traditional therapy models.

So far we've discussed the Helping Gifts that begin to move a teenager from an alcoholic family onto the path of healing and recovery. But the gift of referral will likely have no long-term effect without the next Helping Gift: support.

Support

Support is critical for children of alcoholics' long-term recovery. Any church that wants to play a vital role in helping alcoholic families must commit itself to supporting the families' efforts to get well.

Once a family has said "enough is enough" and has faced the alcoholism, family members can begin the recovery process. But they're still a long way from healing.

Whether the victim is the alcoholic, the alcoholic's spouse or the alcoholic's children, the recovery from the effects of alcoholism is generally believed to take a lifetime. The unhealthy rules, survival roles and alcoholic behavior become so ingrained that it's painstaking to unlearn them. The healthiest alcoholic families view their recovery as a lifelong pursuit. They don't see their situation as hopeless, but they do see it has no quick-and-easy solution.

The changes an alcoholic family undergoes on its road to recovery are radical. The family must rewrite its rules, redefine its roles and restructure its relationships. This can take more time than the typical church is willing to commit in support of a family.

Andrew's family knows the blessing of solid church support during the healing process. When Andrew's father and mother entered a treatment program for alcoholism, the church responded immediately. Andrew, then in junior high, was invited to stay with a church family while his parents went through treatment. The Johnstons welcomed him into their home and, with other church members, made sure Andrew had transportation to the treatment center for every visit and family therapy session.

The first Sunday after his folks' graduation from treatment, Andrew and his family entered the church building and were greeted with hugs and handshakes from nearly everyone. Without being pushy, people offered to help the family whenever they were needed. "Just ask," Andrew heard again and again.

Over the next several months, Andrew's family found that members of the church family were still willing to help when asked. More important, the church still accepted Andrew and his family and made them feel a part of everything, even though the recovery program frequently took them out of midweek and early weekend church events. The church said, in effect, it wanted Andrew's family to attend to its healing first and foremost.

It's no wonder that now, three years later, Andrew's family remains active in the church—and the alcoholism recovery process. As Andrew's story illustrates, youth workers and churches can give several kinds of healthy, meaningful support to recovering COAs and alcoholic families:

Understanding—Learn about their treatment and recovery program. Unless you, the youth group and the congregation understand the recovery process, you're likely to offer more Nice Help than Healthy Help. Once you understand the issues COAs face, you can better support and encourage their healthy recovery.

Before studying the particular recovery process a COA is participating in, get the person's permission. While our understanding is important, even more important is respecting the victims of alcoholism enough to ask how to best support them. Don't just assume—that's what Nice Helpers do. Healthy Helpers ask first.

Once you've talked with the people involved, learn about recovery programs:

● Participate in open meetings. Alcoholics Anonymous (AA) and Al-Anon meetings are structured forums where members share intimately about their progress and problems. Most meetings are closed—only people who are personally working on addictions and alcoholic relationships may attend. But both groups have periodic open meetings. These are excellent opportunities to learn about the recovery process.

I know one minister who makes a special effort to attend open AA meetings with his alcoholic members. He has become so familiar to the alcoholics in his community that he is known as "the alcoholic's pastor." And his efforts have opened significant doors for ministry.

● Ask the COA about the healing process. Many recovering people are eager to share their stories with trustworthy listeners.

● Attend workshops and lectures. Treatment centers frequently offer lectures on alcoholism, family dynamics and recovery. Though usually designed for family members of clients, these programs are open to anyone who's interested. My own recovery as a victim of alcoholism began through a series of these meetings.

● Participate in a victim's treatment program, if appropriate and possible. Most treatment programs offer services to concerned persons—people who may play a significant role in the client's long-term recovery. Since policies vary, consult the victim's alcoholism treatment center for more information.

Shelter—As we've seen, many alcoholic families are also violent families. When victims decide to tell the secret, they may need a safe place to stay for a while. Therefore, the church must know where to send them if safety becomes a concern.

Your ministry and church can be a great asset here. You can identify homes where children and other victims could stay if they seem to be at risk. To learn of such places in the community, contact social service agencies. Keep the phone numbers of such shelters handy.

If no shelters exist in your community or if they are for some reason inaccessible to members of your group and their families, encourage your congregation to work with local agencies to find "safe houses" for victims of domestic violence. Agencies usually have thorough screening processes for these homes. Some members of your congregation might choose to participate in this important ministry.

Patience—The road to recovery for victims of alcoholism is long and difficult. The youth worker and church that patiently stand along that road giving cheers and hugs of encouragement will deeply touch the lives of these people.

As simple as this support may sound, it's not always easy. Several things about recovery can test your patience:

● You'll experience few quick victories. You'll see immediate results only in the earliest stages of healing. After that, recovery becomes a discipline of learning a new lifestyle—which takes years.

● Recovering children of alcoholics will sometimes lose ground. Healing from emotional and psychological wounds frequently means "two steps forward, one step back." And discouragement and frustration frequently accompany the step back. This process can wear down even the most supportive youth worker.

● Finally, our patience may be most severely tested when we see marriages crumble and families split up. The alcoholic family that remains together is the exception, not the rule. Churches have difficulty dealing with this painful experience.

To understand why many alcoholic families dissolve during the healing process, we need to reflect on how relationships work in a dysfunctional family. The alcoholic is not the only addict in the house. Just as the alcoholic is addicted to alcohol, the co-dependent spouse is addicted to controlling the alcoholic.

During recovery, both addicts (the alcoholic and the co-dependent) learn they can live independent of their addictions. The co-dependent spouse may find a new quality of life during recovery. He or she may be unwilling to risk losing this new life by staying in a marriage with a mate who is also predisposed to addiction. As a result, the marriage crumbles.

In some cases, one person begins recovery but the other chooses to stay addicted. This relationship has little chance of long-term success. A split is almost inevitable.

When the church seeks to support alcoholic families in

the midst of crises created by recovery, a whole range of difficult theological and philosophical questions arise—especially in families where not all members are committed to recovery:

1. What does the church believe about marriage? about divorce?

2. Is it better to remain married even though the family will live under extraordinary stress and increased risk?

3. Is it better to divorce for the sake of emotional health, even though it separates children from natural parents?

4. Is it sinful to divorce with the hope of providing long-term health, happiness and well-being for all family members?

5. What would God want for his children who are victims of alcoholism?

6. What is God's healing role in marriages and families that have been torn apart by alcoholism?

I wrestle with these questions every time I work with an alcoholic family on the verge of dissolution. If these questions had simple answers, I wouldn't have to reconsider them each time. Knowing how to respond is difficult, because each circumstance is different.

Openness—Because of the "don't feel" rule, victims of alcoholism need to learn to identify and express feelings. We can support this process by affirming their right to their feelings and by not judging them when they express those feelings.

Our role is to listen without correcting, reprimanding or otherwise trying to change the COAs' feelings. Feelings will change naturally over time as they find appropriate expression. When we try to change another's feelings, we're acting as Nice Helpers who play god.

Many children of alcoholics can express only one emotion: anger. And that comes out only after it has built and festered and grown to explosive proportions. When it blows, it's often inappropriate and ugly.

That was certainly the case when John got angry. For a long time, that was the only emotion he could express. In his anger, he'd swear, scream and sometimes throw things. Fortunately, Russ—John's youth worker—knew how to respond to the outbursts:

● First, he waited until John's outburst had run its course or at least subsided so John could be rational.

● Next, he validated John's anger by agreeing that he had a right to be angry—even angry to the point of hating. He didn't judge John's spirituality on the basis of his behavior during the outburst. "Being angry doesn't make you any less of a person or a Christian," he told John.

● Then, without telling John he was bad, Russ explained there are more appropriate ways to express the anger.

● Finally, he asked John to name any other feelings he felt just underneath the anger.

As John was allowed to express his feelings without fear of rejection, his outbursts diminished. Over time, he was able to identify and express both positive and negative feelings before they sneaked out in unhealthy ways.

If we can accept the idea that *any* feeling can help us be emotionally and spiritually healthy, we can help victims of alcoholism find appropriate ways to express—and even change—their strongest feelings.

A Healthy Family Model

The church has traditionally taught that the family is a child's primary model for values, faith and appropriate behavior. But if this role model is unhealthy, how can we expect its children to be healthy? How can we help the child who has no healthy family model?

We can give Healthy Help to victims of alcoholism by modeling healthy family traits through our youth groups. Youth ministers have long recognized the importance of positive role models for teenagers. Many times the church leaves this responsibility to the youth minister and staff. But a healthy family model that includes the whole youth group becomes a powerful tool in the healing process for children of alcoholics.

Note that I'm recommending a family model in your group, not a model family. There's a difference. A model family is what we imagine to be a perfect family. The phrase conjures images of the Cleavers, Waltons and Huxtables. But these families only exist in the fantasy land of television and in our nostalgic imaginations. The model family is what we'd like all families to be, not what they are. Children of alcoholics don't need model families because they don't need their denial of reality reinforced.

What children of alcoholics need is a family model. They need to discover "normal" or healthy family life in which family members work together to provide unconditional acceptance, emotional validation and nurturing. A healthy family values honesty, patience, listening and fun. A family model sometimes fails, but it recognizes the failure and doesn't judge itself as a result. Instead, it grows from the experience and is confident it will do better with practice.

In her book, *Traits of a Healthy Family*, Dolores Curran provides a wonderful resource about healthy family life. She suggests numerous traits of healthy families. According to her research, a healthy family (among other things):

- communicates and listens;
- affirms and supports one another;
- develops a sense of trust;
- has a sense of play and humor;
- teaches a sense of right and wrong;
- has a balance of interaction among members;
- has a shared religious core; and
- admits to and seeks help with problems.[3]

This abbreviated list shows some of the many characteristics of healthy families that children of alcoholics will never experience at home. It also offers a unique challenge to churches to model these characteristics for these hurting young people.

At first, COAs in your youth group will receive the gift of a family model with some discomfort and anxiety. They aren't used to being in a healthy family. Once they've tried it, though, they usually like it. It becomes an emotionally safe place for them to live. In some instances it can become their "family of choice," the group of people they choose to be with because it provides acceptance, nurturing and validation.

Many recovering victims of alcoholism make a 12-Step support group their family of choice because it meets their needs. When your youth group provides the Helping Gift of a family model, it may also become the family of choice for many hurting teenagers.

This book frequently refers to family rules that result from dysfunction. But don't conclude that family rules are necessarily unimportant or always bad. All families have and need rules to function in healthy ways. The difference is that some rules hurt the people who follow them, while others help.

You can help your youth group become a healthy family model—and a family of choice for hurting kids—by helping it develop some healthy "family rules." These rules should:

- protect the dignity of each family member;
- teach respect for personal boundaries and confidences;
- build trust;
- encourage honesty at all levels and in all expressions;
- validate feelings; and
- encourage unconditional acceptance of one another.

Establishing rules for a healthy group involves more than announcing, "Hey, gang, it's like this. We now have some new rules, and here they are." Rather, allow your group to define and declare its own rules based on what it thinks makes families healthy.

To start this process, tell the group about healthy family functioning. Once group members grasp the information, they can begin writing the group's own rules. Encourage the group to do this in a planning meeting or at a retreat.

Once the rules have been agreed upon, make sure everyone knows them, their purpose and the consequences for disregarding them. Ask group members to commit to living by the healthy rules. Then commit yourself to live by the group's rules too.

I've found this process isn't as difficult as it might seem. What's difficult is staying out of the way to let the group develop its own rules. These rules might address issues of being honest with each other, expressing feelings openly, and being vulnerable.

Establishing healthy, nurturing rules for your group may seem insignificant. But it represents a major step toward creating a family model for its members. As your group begins to operate under healthy rules, COAs will be attracted to it as a safe, nurturing place—a place like home ought to be.

A Challenge to the Church

Awareness, identification, intervention, referral, support and a healthy family model are six Helping Gifts children of alcoholics need for recovery. They often have to go to agencies and groups outside the church to receive these gifts.

While I'm glad these gifts are available, I'm disappointed, angered and saddened that the church has—in general—been stingy toward the victims of alcoholism. My dream and challenge is that churches will become places of Healthy Help where children of alcoholics will find no shortage of Helping Gifts. For when we give these gifts, we earn the right to present to children of alcoholics the final and most important Helping Gift: hope. We'll examine this gift in Chapter 9.

Work It Out

1. Brainstorm with other youth leaders ways your youth program can offer the six Helping Gifts (awareness, identification, intervention, referral, support and a healthy family model) mentioned in this chapter and Chapter 7. Then select the ideas you believe would work best with your group. How can you incorporate these into your existing program?

2. Most helping professionals work under ethical guidelines that outline clients' rights, such as the right to confidentiality. However, helping professionals also have a duty to warn and protect when they know their client or another person named by the client is in immediate danger. What guidance does your church give concerning these issues? If it gives no guidance, what is your ethical code, and how have you formed it? With others on the church staff, decide how to respond when the issue of confidentiality arises.

3. What experience have you had related to intervention? What was painful about the experience? How did the pain enhance or detract from the healing? Do you think healing could take place without the pain?

4. Evaluate your referral list. Does it include individuals who meet the criteria listed on page 131? If not, begin building an appropriate list so it will be available when needed.

5. Evaluate yourself and your church in the areas of support. For each area, give yourself a 5 if you feel confident in it and a 1 if you feel you haven't developed this area at all. Choose one area where you feel you need the most work, and brainstorm ways to improve.

a. Understanding and knowledge of the
   treatment program   5   4   3   2   1
b. Ability to provide shelter for victims
   of alcoholism if needed   5   4   3   2   1
c. Patience to help victims through
   long-term recovery   5   4   3   2   1
d. Openness to and affirmation of ex-
   pressed feelings   5   4   3   2   1

6. Would you say your youth group is a healthy family model? If so, why? If not, what areas need improvement? Think of ways to address these issues in your group.

Endnotes

[1]Conrad Bergendoff, *Pastoral Care for Alcoholism: An Introduction* (Center City, MN: Hazelden Educational Materials, 1981), 16.

[2]Will Maloney, *Chemical Dependency Treatment Programs: A Guide to Referral* (Center City, MN: Hazelden Educational Materials, 1987).

[3]Dolores Curran, *Traits of a Healthy Family* (San Francisco: Ballantine Books, 1983).

CHAPTER 9

A Message of Hope

Words COAs Need to Hear From the Church

"**W**hen you wish upon a star . . ."

Now an adult, Rick still gets a lump in his throat every time he hears that popular film song. He vividly remembers the first time he heard Jiminy Cricket sing it in *Pinocchio.* His mom had taken Rick to the movie to escape his drunk, abusive father. His childlike faith immediately accepted the promise of the song as true: "When you wish upon a star . . . your dreams come true."

On the ride home, Rick watched out the window for the brightest star he could see. When he found it he made his wish. It didn't come true. That night's beating fractured no bones, but it did break Rick's spirit.

Wishing and Hoping

If wishes came true, we wouldn't need to help kids in alcoholic families. Their problems would have vanished long ago. They each wish for a parent miraculously to become sober and sane. They each wish God—or anybody—would swoop into their home and steal them away to a place of happiness and peace. They each wish for a new life in a new place with a new family. Sometimes they even wish so hard that their fantasies become more real than their reality.

While wishes provide a sweet escape, wishful thinkers don't really expect their wishes to come true. That's the nature of wishes. If we really believed our wish were possible, it wouldn't be a wish. It would be hope.

Unlike a wish, hope isn't based in fantasy but in reality. It acknowledges the result without diminishing the process, the destination without foregoing the journey. It's the heart of Romans 8:28: "And we know that in all things God works for the good of those who love him, who have been called according to his purpose."

For children of alcoholics, hope is an invitation to believe: to believe they can do more than just survive; to believe change is possible for themselves—even if the family never changes; to believe they can discover a healthy, sane family of choice; to believe God really does care and is willing to help.

Giving Messages of Hope

Hope is perhaps the greatest Helping Gift we can give children of alcoholics. However, delivering a message of hope isn't easy. While children of alcoholics are full of wishes, most feel hopeless. It may take months—even years—for a COA to begin hoping.

We give Healthy Help to victims of alcoholism when we give the Helping Gift of hope frequently and regularly. It needs to be like a series of affirming notes, not just one long letter. Let's look at what those notes need to say:

"You're not alone." Many children from alcoholic families hide in silent pain because they see themselves as unique. They need to hear that their problem is common. Recovering children of alcoholics frequently say, "I didn't realize anyone else could know what my life was like." When they begin to believe others like them exist, they each gain confidence to tell their own story. They break the "don't talk" rule and open themselves for healing.

Accepting this message takes more than statistics. Victims of alcoholism need to see and hear from one or more other children of alcoholics. Thus it's important to help COAs in your group contact others who've been through the same experience and are being healed. Invite recovering children of alcoholics to tell their stories to your group. And encourage COA group members to attend Alateen or Al-Anon support group meetings.

"You didn't cause it." Children of alcoholics need to know they didn't cause the alcoholic's addiction. The addiction is coincidental to their presence in the family, not related to it.

This message is crucial. Many children have been blamed outright for the family's alcohol problem. And even if no one has ever directly blamed a particular child of an alcoholic, he or she feels the blame nonetheless. The child's potential to recover from the effects of alcoholism depends on his or her ability to shake feelings of blame.

Many children of alcoholics will have to hear "You didn't cause it" hundreds of times before they can say, "I didn't cause it." Then, after they've said it to themselves an infinite number of times, they may begin to believe it.

"You won't cure or control it." Children of alcoholics find ingenious ways to try to keep an alcoholic from drinking. I used food coloring and water to dilute my dad's Jim Beam. Another COA rearranged her mom's booze stashes by putting empties where the full ones were so her mom would think the booze was all gone.

Others hide checkbooks, change balances or steal cash from pocketbooks so there won't be money for liquor. Some use emotional manipulation, such as angry threats and intimidation, uncontrolled "loony" behavior, and sobbing pleas for sobriety.

Children of alcoholics go to nearly any length to keep booze from taking over an otherwise loving parent. They really think they can control, maybe even cure, the alcoholic. The wishful fantasy slows their own healing.

When they understand the nature of addiction, children of alcoholics can begin letting go of their desire to control or cure the problem. As they each see their alcoholic parent as an addict, they can more easily see that their efforts to fix the parent are in vain.

"Your life doesn't have to stay as it is." These words are an invitation to believe change is possible. But it needs to be clear who must make the changes.

Cheri, a college sophomore, recently began facing the pain of victimization by alcoholism. She has grown tremendously in just a few months. Because of her honest confrontation of her own past, her life embodies healing and the hope of recovery.

However, Cheri's recovery nearly ended at the beginning. She tried to share her discoveries with her family members, but they rejected everything Cheri said. They nearly even rejected her for raising the alcohol issue.

Cheri was devastated. But through a counselor and some friends, she recognized her recovery couldn't depend upon the family's response. Even if her family chose to stay unhealthy, she didn't have to.

Children from alcoholic families need to understand their healing cannot—indeed, must not—depend on whether their families receive help. The family may never get any better. But COAs need to learn that they don't have to feel stuck in the way things are. While pain and fear sometimes occur, they don't have to be ever-present. Instead these children can be liberated to experience the abundant life God desires for each person.

"Live and let live" is a motto frequently heard in 12-Step group meetings and chemical dependency treatment centers. It reminds victims of alcoholism of a simple truth: You can only be responsible for one person—yourself. Change is possible. But we have the ability and responsibility to change only ourselves. We can't change others, no matter how much we love them or hurt for them in their pain.

"Jesus Christ can become your greatest source of healing, strength and support." This message's implications are clear. When COA teenagers consider Christ's offer to become their Greatest Source, they're challenged to turn their life and recovery over to him.

I prefer to use non-traditional language when communicating with COAs and their families about Jesus Christ. When I do use traditional language, I carefully define it. I believe fresh, descriptive names for Christ and God communicate most clearly by counteracting any negative images of God victims of alcoholism may have already formed.

Traditional names for God have a rich and powerful meaning for many Christians. However, certain names may have connotations that prevent some children of alcoholics from wanting Jesus Christ to be part of their recovery. Consider these examples:

● Since children of alcoholics would like to be rescued from their families, the name "Savior" can suggest to them a Superman Jesus who will snatch them away to safety. When this fantasy doesn't happen they can become disillusioned.

● The name "Lord" can have a frightening connotation to victims, particularly in cases of abuse or incest. Lord conveys the ideas of authority, mastery and power. If, as children, COAs had to hide from those who had authority (parents), they will unlikely be drawn to one who is called Lord for fear of the same treatment.

● This same problem can evoke negative responses to calling God "Father." Children whose only earthly father is abusive, threatening and authoritarian have difficulty understanding God as a loving heavenly Father.

When we look in scripture, we discover that God's people have used a variety of names to describe their God. Indeed, scripture includes more than 700 names for God. Each name has had particular significance and meaning to different people.

In sharing the gospel of grace with children of alcoholics, I use fresh names that still accurately reflect God's nature. Many names for God and Jesus in the Bible can be particularly meaningful to COAs—Counselor (Isaiah 9:6), Friend (Luke 7:34), Sunrise (Luke 1:77-79). This last example is a beautiful scripture to share with those in need of healing and peace. Both the name and the scripture offer the promise of a new day of healing.

Whatever language you use, the goal is to communicate God's desire to be part of the teenager's life and healing. Because a COA's self-esteem is often so badly damaged, victims of alcoholism need to hear over and over the message of God's unconditional love.

"God loves and accepts you just as you are." After being disgusted by many dumb bumper stickers on our nation's highways, I finally saw one I really liked. It had the name of a church in small letters across the top. But just below, in large letters, it read: "Come as you are . . . you'll be loved!"

COAs desperately need to hear that message from churches. However, it's a difficult message for them to receive. COAs are often kept from experiencing God's grace by one thing: a fantasy that they have the power to control things. Until they accept their inability to fix even themselves, they can't know the liberation of grace.

The experience of God's grace eluded me for more than 30 years. Only when I was hospitalized in a drug-and-alcohol treatment unit was I forced to choose between God's grace and my own sense of power.

I remember it as if it were last week.

I entered treatment on a Monday morning. My life had become so painful that the unresolved emotional garbage I had as a COA forced me into the hospital. Arriving at 7 a.m., I was eager to start. This place held the promise of easing my hurt.

Following an interview and examination by the staff physician, I was admitted with a diagnosis of "stress reaction disorder." The diagnosis satisfied my insurance company so I wouldn't have to pay the $250-plus per day myself. Actually, the diagnosis was another name for being a severely co-dependent adult child of an alcoholic.

I arrived in my room and immediately began working on my treatment assignments. I wanted to do well, since the price of failure was high. It could mean the loss of my family and my career—not to mention the insurance payments for the treatment.

Following dinner that evening, I attended my first Step Study session where I was introduced to Step 1 of the 12-Step approach. Before I could move to Step 2, I had to explain to the leader's satisfaction that I understood being powerless.

"No sweat," I thought.

When the leader asked, "Tom, what are you powerless over?" I began to rattle off everything I could think of: God, animals, nature, the expansion of McDonald's corporation, Walter Payton's retirement from football, my dog and on and on.

She didn't seem satisfied. "Are you powerless over people, or do you believe you can control them?" she prodded.

"Well," I answered, "I can usually get them to do what I want."

That confession was a tactical blunder, but it triggered my recovery. She sent me away that first night with an assignment to read about powerlessness and to think through my understanding of it.

On the second day I returned to my Step Study to face the same questions. This time I rattled through the same list I used the night before and added, "And I suppose people, too."

I expected the instructor to congratulate me and invite me to progress to Step 2. Wrong. She asked, "What else are you powerless over?"

I was stuck and speechless. "What else is there?" I wondered aloud.

"Think about it some more," she said and sent me away with the same assignment. I left embarrassed and frustrated.

The third day found me wondering if I could complete the treatment. My doubt was compounded by a frightening experience during a morning group therapy session— another patient was confronted about being dishonest and playing "mind games." Her failure to admit what she was doing resulted in her immediate dismissal from the treatment program. She was packed and gone in 20 minutes.

That evening I attended Step Study as required. Again I was asked about my powerlessness. And again I ran through my list. One more time the leader told me it wasn't complete. My frustration and irritation became obvious in my manner and voice. My mind began to whirl with visions of that morning's confrontation. Only now, in place of the woman, I saw myself.

In a controlled rage I asked, "Just what do you people want from me?"

"We just want you to understand what powerlessness means."

"How can I understand it if you won't tell me what it is?"

A third time I went away with the same assignment but with more frustration and anger.

The fourth morning was horrible. I awoke to 6 a.m. aerobics with a migraine headache and nausea. The leaders let me skip a one-hour lecture to lie down. But they wouldn't give me aspirin. I couldn't believe I was in a hospital full of medicine and I couldn't even have aspirin.

After lunch I met a new patient, Flo. She seemed like a typical American grandmother. And she definitely seemed out of place among the alcoholics, drug addicts and codependents at the large afternoon session.

I was shocked when the staff facilitator went right to work on Flo. "Flo, why are you here?"

Within minutes it was obvious to all that Flo was keeping a secret. Despite the facilitator's best efforts and pressure from the group, Flo never said why she was there—though she told lots of inconsistent stories.

After a short restroom break, the group reconvened for a second hour. Once again the facilitator went after Flo. This time she asked, "Flo, who did you call during break?" This confirmed my suspicion that the facilitator knew something we didn't. Flo denied using the phone. Then the facilitator returned to the original question, "Why are you here, Flo?"

What followed was an intense game of verbal chess between Flo and the group. Flo became nervous. At one point she tried to pour a drink of water, but was shaking so badly she missed the cup and poured it on the floor.

"Whew, is she shook!" I thought to myself as I lifted my coffee cup to take a sip. Then I noticed how nervous I was. I was shaking so badly I had to use both hands to steady my cup. The game ended when the facilitator gave Flo a choice: Either tell the truth about herself or leave. Flo left, only four hours after she checked in.

After Flo left, the facilitator explained that Flo was no stranger to the unit. She had been through alcohol treatment before and had come back today by court order because of drunk driving.

I was still shaking when I went to Step Study that evening. The facilitator asked again. I listed again. She smiled, told me I was still missing the point, and sent me out to think more. I was too tired, too frightened, too sick, too numb to be angry. My head was pounding. I walked to my room, stood at my window overlooking the Mississippi River and sobbed.

Feeling like a total failure, I resigned myself to the same fate as Flo and the other woman. It was only a matter of time—maybe tomorrow—till they'd figure out I couldn't make it. I didn't have what it took to complete the program. It seemed so ironic that I was just trying to become a better person, and I couldn't even do that.

As I was getting ready for bed, a nearly audible voice spoke to me. "Tom, read Romans 7."

"Great," I thought. "Not only am I failing, now I'm hearing a voice and it's telling me to read the Bible passage I hate most." I ignored the voice.

Still it kept repeating, "Read Romans 7."

Finally, when it was obvious that the voice and my headache wouldn't let me sleep, I threw off my covers, grabbed my Bible and angrily read Romans 7 as quickly and sarcastically as I could. When I finished I shouted, "There! So shut up!" and slammed the Bible hard onto the desk. Then I fell into a deep, peaceful sleep.

At 4 a.m. I awoke to the sound of serenity. My headache was gone. I wasn't nauseated. I felt hopeful and re-laxed. For the first time in my life, I understood Romans 7 and what it meant to be powerless. It was incredible!

To be powerless not only meant I couldn't control the items on my Step Study list, but it also meant I had no power over myself. I always knew and believed I couldn't keep myself from doing wrong. But it had never occurred to me that I didn't have the power to make myself do good, to be a better person. In fact, I had always prided myself in the sincerity and intensity of my efforts.

Now I knew I couldn't overcome my problem alone. I had no power to do what only God could do. My only hope was the same as Paul's: "What a wretched man I am! Who will rescue me from this body of death? Thanks be to God—through Jesus Christ our Lord!" (Romans 7:24-25).

The fifth day of treatment was the day I stopped trying. I stopped trying to succeed in the treatment program. I stopped trying to be a better Christian, husband and father. I stopped trying to be a better youth minister. I stopped try-ing to fix my alcoholic family. I stopped trying to make my-self acceptable to God. I relaxed into the waiting arms of my Higher Power and Greatest Source: Jesus Christ.

Ultimately all victims of alcoholism can find hope in ex-periencing grace. As I learned, knowing *about* grace is not enough. Only when grace is experienced in the heart can the victims of alcoholism surrender themselves and begin healing.

This surrender isn't hopelessly giving in to the addic-tion or its hurtful results. The surrender is a hopeful ex-change of our own insufficient power for the all-sufficient power of God. That power is the power for growth, recov-ery and healing. God's empowerment through our power-lessness is the message of hope.

Healing Through Powerlessness

The Helping Gift of hope isn't the church's exclusive property. Others can give it as well. Yet no other group has greater potential for offering this message than the church. Despite its quirks, blunders and sins, the church has a message of hope for today. And people in pain are among those who most quickly come to us for help.

Our message of hope can be based in Nice Help or Healthy Help. It's easier for us to give Nice Help, and the victim even feels good for a while. Yet our Nice Help is a temporary binding that makes the wound worse. Only Healthy Help—rooted in a grace-filled message of hope—can provide the catalyst for complete and lasting healing.

Work It Out

1. Review the messages of hope in this chapter. List ways you can communicate each one verbally and non-verbally.

2. What other hopeful messages would you want to communicate to children of alcoholics? Add these to your list, along with ways to communicate them.

3. What's your personal story of discovering and experiencing God's grace? Have you shared it with anyone recently? Write it, then read it to someone or a group you trust. Consider sharing it with your youth group as a testimony to the truth of God's grace.

CHAPTER 10

Wounded Healers

How Adult Children of Alcoholics Minister to Teenagers

"**H**ow many of you are children of alcoholics?"

With the exception of three or four, all hands went up.

"Now, how many of you COAs are in helping professions?"

All but a dozen or so hands ascended.

These questions were posed to about 80 patients at the treatment center where I received help. The facilitator asked people to raise their hands to make a point to me. She wanted me to know I wasn't alone. Then she offered me this challenge, "Tom, if you share your story with others when you get out of here, you'll be surprised how many children of alcoholics work in the church."

That wasn't an easy challenge for me to accept, because it required a level of self-disclosure I had never known. But my curiosity eventually compelled me to accept both the challenge and its consequences. I began to share with other ministers.

I was shocked to learn how right the facilitator was.

I really don't know the number of youth workers who grew up in alcoholic families. A therapist friend once told me she attended a conference where someone reported that

80 percent of all church professionals are children of alcoholics. That figure is similar to the findings of Episcopal priest Stephen Apthorp. He writes that "a show of hands [at regional training seminars] has indicated that 80 percent of clergy present have come from families debilitated by substance abuse."[1]

While I'm not aware of any scientific data to substantiate these figures, this informal data indicates that many pastors and youth workers are products of alcoholic and otherwise dysfunctional homes. Often they were Family Heroes who tried to fix and/or care for other family members who seemed more needy than themselves. As adults they were drawn to church careers because they found themselves comfortable as professional caretakers.

But many of these COAs are people in pain who turn to youth work as an opportunity to grasp the sense of wholeness and worth that has always been just beyond their reach. They have an overdeveloped sense of responsibility, an intense need to be needed and a learned talent for giving Nice Help. Yet many remain unaware of the wounds and needs that profoundly influence their ministry.

This chapter features some of the insights and struggles COA youth workers face in their ministries.

To Trust or Not to Trust

I'm a good organizer and planner. While my skills are valuable, little do people realize these were acquired as a result of my inability to trust others and my fear of being out of control.

Like most kids growing up in alcoholic families, I learned that I was the most trustworthy person I knew. That distrust of others bred a need to control. For most of my adult years, I've tried obsessively to be in total control of my life and work, because I didn't feel I could trust others with any responsibilities.

Whenever my youth group would plan meetings or events, I usually had a secret backup plan—just in case the people responsible didn't follow through. The backup plan would be as simple as a spare package of cookies in my car or as complex as a whole meeting outline—complete with props, materials and special effects. Two or three times I actually substituted my own backup plans even though the people in charge had done their work. I said I felt my plans would be more effective. Wasn't that a wonderfully affirming message I sent the organizers?

Do you know how exhausting it is to try to control everything? I didn't notice it much when I was in my teens and 20s and had boundless energy and a simpler life. But as I faced increased responsibilities in my career and family, my body began to lose its youthful energy. It took burning out three times in six years to make me realize I couldn't do it all myself anymore.

In my recovery, I learned that my problem with trust and control is a confusion of power. An inflated sense of self-power had, since childhood, made it difficult for me to see the difference between God and me. I acted as I thought God should act. When God seemed not to care about Dad's drinking, I concluded he was one more person I couldn't trust. So I had to take charge.

I still struggle with the need to control. I keep letting go of things I've tried to control. I work to trust others with responsibilities I once clung to.

In the process, I've developed close friendships with a couple of people I know can—and will—confront me when they see me inappropriately taking charge. My Adult Children of Alcoholics (ACOA) support group is also a good place to receive feedback. I make myself accountable to these people, yet I don't hold them responsible for my decisions and actions.

Now I am finding joy in seeing co-workers' excitement as they take charge of projects. I also experience a new sense of satisfaction in teaching others and seeing young people grow when I set them free to plan, organize and lead their own gatherings—without my backup plans.

Addicted to Helping

Margie laughed at herself as she told me how she would try to help kids: "This crazy image comes to mind of me chasing a girl across a field and making a flying tackle. Then I'd sit on top of her, pin her shoulders to the ground, stare her down and say, 'Look, I know you need help and I'm going to give it to you whether you want it or not.'" Margie never really got this bold. "But I was close to it!" she confesses.

In truth, Margie was obsessed with helping kids.

Margie prided herself for usually knowing about a teenager's problem before anyone told her about it. Margie would work hard to become friends with group members. She attended their ball games, concerts and plays. She knew their families and their friends (her two main sources of information). She even ate school lunches with her kids.

To most people, Margie was just being a conscientious youth worker. She cared deeply about young people and wanted to help them when appropriate. But the "appropriate" part caused Margie problems.

For Margie it wasn't enough to be aware of the teenagers' needs and problems. She tried to help them before they were ready to receive help. Sometimes she tried to help them using "covert operations." If she noticed a group member who didn't have many friends, she'd secretly ask other kids to befriend the person. When her efforts were exposed, kids often felt angry, manipulated and hurt.

While her covert efforts hurt kids, her overt attempts frequently frightened them away. She'd tell them what she knew; she'd say how she could help; then she'd start to work. She even repeatedly called kids to check whether they were following through on advice they only reluctantly received. Even when kids told her directly they didn't want or need her help, she proceeded anyway—believing they really couldn't know what was best.

Her obsessive-compulsive behavior created crises in Margie's ministry. One or two kids and their parents would get upset with her. They'd accuse her of interfering and tell her to keep out of their business. Margie would take their criticism as rejection, announce that the church didn't appreciate her work, and resign. Until she got help, Margie never lasted more than 24 months at a church.

Margie faced her problem when she dared to stay with one church longer than two years. When the crisis came, the staff confronted her and committed themselves to her support if she'd get help. A counselor encouraged her to attend both Al-Anon and ACOA meetings.

At the ACOA support group, Margie learned how she had been affected by her mother's alcoholism. As a child, she had been obsessed with helping her mom stop drinking. Then when Margie was 14, her mother died in a car accident—the result of drunk driving. Margie had failed to save her mom. The ACOA group helped her realize she was still trying to save her mom by "rescuing" group members.

At first Margie thought it was stupid to attend Al-Anon meetings. After all, her mother had been dead for years. But after a few meetings, Margie began to see wisdom in her counselor's advice. She learned how to "detach with love" from her youth group members. She learned that other people's problems weren't her fault and she couldn't fix them.

She began applying Al-Anon slogans to her life and ministry: "Easy does it"; "Live and let live"; and "Let go and let God." Surprisingly, she found herself less obsessed with other people's problems and more able to let people ask for her help rather then force it on them.

Margie is still in youth ministry. In fact, she has stayed at the same place for nearly nine years. She's also more effective than ever, deeply loved by her group members and their families for her caring, sensitive ministry.

Did You Call, God?

I never seriously questioned my calling to youth ministry until I read Gordon MacDonald's book, *Ordering Your Private World*. MacDonald contrasts a called person and a driven person. He suggests people become driven when they're raised in environments where:

- Affirmation and approval are rarely given.
- They experience shame, deprivation and embarrassment.
- Other family members model drivenness.[2]

As I read MacDonald's description, I found myself more closely identifying with the driven person. Then I was struck with a terrible thought: Am I called by God to youth ministry, or am I merely acting out an old, unhealthy alcoholic family role?

I've learned that my question is common among recovering adult children of alcoholics. One COA minister writes, "I have realized that throughout my ministry I have accepted calls to congregations which replicate the dynamics of the alcoholic family in which I was raised."[3]

Stephen Apthorp indicates that my question nags many ministers who grew up in alcoholic families: "For many this history was a determining factor in the decision to enter the ministry."[4]

To illustrate the difference between being called and being driven into ministry, consider the cases of two youth workers, Randy and John. Both believe themselves to be called to youth ministry. Randy is a child of an alcoholic. John grew up in a seemingly healthy family.

Randy's alcoholic parents were frequently unpredictable and inconsistent. He grew up guessing at everything and hoping he was doing the "right" thing. According to his parents, he usually guessed wrong. They'd curse and call him horrible names whenever he failed to do what they thought he should do instinctively. Randy began to work for their approval and acceptance. He always hoped they would someday say: "Randy, we love you. You're okay just the way you are."

John's family had clear rules, and he received regular affirmation from parents and siblings. He can't ever remember being shamed or called a foul name by either parent. He was always recognized for doing his best.

Randy learned to try to make others happy.

John learned to be happy with himself.

With this background, can you imagine how differently each might live out his youth ministry call?

John receives and assimilates input about his ministry from church officials, teenagers, group members' parents and his own understanding. He gives the greatest weight to his own ideas as he is led by God's Spirit. This way John feels he can be clear about his calling and who he is.

Randy receives input from the same sources. But he gives greater weight to everyone else's opinions. In fact, he never considers the value of his own ideas. Randy frantically tries to please everyone despite conflicting ideas and expectations. As a result, others' wishes shape his ministry much more than his sense of God's calling.

The teenagers want more fun events. But neither the parents nor the church believes "fun" is a valid purpose for youth group meetings. The kids like to meet Randy informally with their friends. Yet the parents complain that he always seems to be "just hanging around" and never working.

Randy is so driven to please everyone that he doesn't have time to evaluate his ministry in light of his calling. Sadly, even when he does have time, he won't be able to do it because he has never learned how to be his own person, to identify his needs and to love himself.

Randy strives to be perfect. He remembers perfection being his childhood standard for judging whether he was an okay person. If his efforts didn't satisfy all expectations, they weren't good enough—and neither was he. He never outgrew that perspective. Instead, he carried it with him into adulthood and ministry.

The church is a good place for perfectionists. The work is a challenge, and the church usually gets hard workers for little pay. It seems like a perfect match.

Until . . .

Perfectionism drives you crazy. The perfectionist is stressed not only by the work but also by the fear that someone might find a flaw. The perfectionist is even more stressed when working with other people, because another person with a free will may not always give in to the perfectionist's plan.

As a perfectionist, I would almost explode when my precisely scheduled events were "ruined" because a group of kids—even a single teenager—wasn't on time. I'd leave meetings frustrated and angry because what I had planned to be a meaningful, serious meeting erupted into hilarity because of one teenager's overactive sense of humor.

In the height of my perfectionism, I competed only with myself. Each activity I planned had to be better than the last. Every time I counseled a kid, I had to see some improvement in my skills. If I dealt with the same teenager repeatedly, I had to feel my growth as a counselor was staying ahead of his growth as a client. I gave myself impossible goals—with impossible price tags.

To deal with my perfectionism, I've had to learn to do what is most difficult for me: to trust God. I try to keep this perspective each day: Do what I can with the time, resources and information I have, but leave the results to God. This has relieved a lot of the pressure.

The most satisfactory answer I've found to my personal question of "called" versus "driven" is that I'm called to youth ministry but, for most of my career, I've lived out that calling as a driven, compulsive person.

Again, my recovery program and accountability to special friends have helped me identify when I'm acting in a driven, perfectionist manner. As a result, I can perform my ministry today as I believe God intended when he originally called me to youth work.

Love, Sex and Youth Work

Ron's dad was an alcoholic. Ron internalized the survival rules and roles. He kept the family secret and endured his childhood by burying his feelings deep inside.

He also learned to relate to women through his dad's example. When his dad was sober, he could be kind, gentle, caring and affectionate toward Ron's mother—especially when he wanted sex. But when his dad was drunk and wanted sex, he wouldn't take time for all the niceties. Years later Ron realized he had actually witnessed—on at least two occasions—his drunk dad raping his mother.

Because of this pattern, Ron learned to equate love with sex and to see women as objects for sexual gratification. But since Ron was a gentle, compassionate and genuinely caring man (like his sober dad), he attracted Joan to marry him.

Despite their best efforts, Ron and Joan's marriage was always difficult. Joan could never seem to get through the protective wall that surrounded Ron. She knew *about* him, but she never really knew him.

Joan also felt "used" by Ron. She couldn't shake the awful feeling Ron had married her out of convenience. She got the dirty jobs, while Ron did what was most important to him. Even worse, Joan began to feel like Ron's concubine rather than his wife.

In time their relationship became cool and distant. When Joan began to reject his sexual advances, Ron started to think she didn't love him anymore. So Ron came on even stronger. Joan's rejection was just as strong. And so the sexual war escalated until one day Ron nearly forced himself on Joan—just as he'd seen his dad do to his mom.

That battle frightened both Ron and Joan. Joan decided sex wouldn't be a part of their marriage for a long time. Ron decided to stop demanding it and accept a new lifestyle of celibacy. Both felt hurt and unloved.

About the time Ron and Joan were adjusting to this change, a teenager from Ron's youth group requested counseling. In their first session Ron found himself stricken by the depth of Sherry's problems and needs. They decided to meet regularly for several weeks, then to assess her progress.

Within months, a relationship formed with Sherry that was everything Ron thought his marriage should be. It was easy to care about Sherry and her problems. He could listen to her forever. Ron also began to see that Sherry could return the same kindness and compassion he gave her. Within a year, they had exchanged "I love yous" and started a sexual relationship.

The story's outcome is one that's too common in youth ministry. Ron lost his job at the church and his career in youth ministry. He and Joan divorced shortly afterward. Ron and Sherry left the community together, but their relationship lasted only six years. Then they too had problems, and Ron turned to Nicky for "love."

I share this story because youth workers from alcoholic homes may be at higher risk for inappropriate sexual relationships. COA youth workers—and others who grew up in dysfunctional families—need to know they may be particularly vulnerable to this problem.

I believe three primary reasons lie behind this tendency:

● First, children of alcoholics often don't know how to build a healthy marriage. Alcoholic family rules may be good for survival, but you can't build a healthy marriage if one partner won't talk, trust or express feelings.

● Second, unless they receive help before marriage, COAs are likely to recreate unhealthy families. If their marriages are shaky, COAs are particularly vulnerable in professions like youth ministry where they are frequently surrounded by attractive young men and women.

● Finally, COA youth workers are emotionally needy people. If they're not aware of their own emotional deprivation and its pain, they'll continue to try to compensate for their loss. This search can lead them into inappropriate relationships with group members. Their relationships can involve excessive helping, overidentification or extreme emotional attachment. These are only a few of the ways COA youth workers may try to make up for the unconditional love, acceptance and security they didn't receive in their alcoholic families.

Wounds

I've spent most of my youth ministry career as a "walking wounded." As a result, I've bled profusely over the kids

I've tried to help, often obscuring their problems and denying their pain. My unconscious motivation was to find healing for myself by taking care of others.

In my quest for my own healing, I was never able to be fully present for any hurting teenager.

Because I had never talked about my deepest hurts, I couldn't feel comfortable listening to kids speak of theirs.

Because I denied and ignored my own feelings, I couldn't understand and validate theirs.

Because I had never walked with Jesus Christ through my own pain, I couldn't show young people the way through theirs.

Because I couldn't honestly face my own secrets, I couldn't challenge kids to face theirs.

Ironically, because I deceived myself into thinking I was being a wounded healer, I couldn't see what they knew: that I was only a walking wounded.

Today, by the grace of God, I really am—and am becoming—a wounded healer. The idea of being a wounded healer has appealed to me from the first time I learned about Henri Nouwen's book with that title.[5] "That makes sense," I said to myself. "That's what I want to be."

Yet it wasn't so simple. Little did I know the true price of becoming a wounded healer: admitting my own woundedness.

That admission is difficult for us to make in ministry because of the fear of disapproval. "If I admit my wounds to God and my church," we wonder to ourselves, "won't they think I'm unfit to work with kids? Won't this confession disqualify me until I get my life together again and am healed?"

There's no answer to relieve the struggle of that question. All you can do is decide. You can run from the fear by remaining among the walking wounded—like so many pastors and youth ministers do—or you can face the fear and choose the life of a wounded healer. The fellowship may be smaller, but it's certainly sweeter.

In my decision to choose the life of a wounded healer,

I've found several things to be true:

I am truly being healed. God hasn't abandoned me to the pain of my wounds; nor am I immune to hurt and further injury. But while I was among the walking wounded, these hurts simply gaped and became infected. Today they are bound one at a time. The healing may leave a scar, but even the scar reminds me that I have been wounded and healed to be stronger than ever.

I am becoming a Healthy Helper. You can't admit woundedness without being confronted by the stark reality that you're human. This discovery is a basic step toward becoming a Healthy Helper who is willing and able to confront problems in a loving, direct and helpful way. I've found admitting my woundedness hasn't disqualified me from youth work. In fact, it has made me more effective. Though I'm not perfect and must tend to my own wounds daily, my ministry has been strengthened.

I no longer cower before the fear of disapproval. I now know with confidence that God doesn't disapprove of my woundedness. How could he? It was for my wounds that Jesus Christ lived, died and lives again. Indeed, God can't approve me as righteous until I admit my woundedness.

But what about my church? If the price of its approval is for me to deny my wounds, then that price is too high. I have decided to invest my life in service with people who can accept me in the same way God does: lovingly, unconditionally and with grace.

From One Youth Worker to All Others

The young people with whom we minister deserve Healthy Help from us regardless of our family background and our personal struggles. In reality, all youth workers face many of the struggles described in this chapter, though COA youth workers may have a greater struggle with them than others.

However, none of these issues necessarily prevents us from being Healthy Helpers. Regardless of your wounds or struggles, I hope for you:

 ● the experience of God's grace, that you may know God's approval of you as righteous, good and acceptable in his sight.

 ● the experience of God's love, that you may know the joy that comes from the nurturing of a Caring Parent.

 ● the experience of God's comfort, that you may know the healing he gives as you bring even your deepest wounds to him.

 ● the experience of God's presence, that you will no longer know a frightened child's terror.

 ● the experience of God's peace, that you may be set free to become a Healthy Helper and give to others what you waited so long to receive.

Work It Out

1. If you aren't sure whether you're an adult child of an alcoholic, take the "Children of Alcoholics Screening Test" on page 114. If you discover that you may be, see a trained counselor and join an Adult Children of Alcoholics group in your community.

2. Do you agree with the perception that many, if not most, ministers are from alcoholic or otherwise dysfunctional homes? If not, why? If so, how does this perspective affect your view of the ministry?

3. Think of instances in your own experience when you've had trouble trusting people because you felt the need to control. If you see an inability to trust and a desire to control as problems, think of concrete ways you can begin trusting people in your ministry and family with responsibilities.

4. Do you feel like you're obsessed with helping kids? If so, is the help you give them Healthy or just Nice? How can you shift from Nice Help to Healthy Help?

5. With which of the two youth ministers described in the section Did You Call, God? do you most closely identify? If you identify more with Randy, get a copy of Mac-

Donald's book to help you examine your call and motivation in ministry.

6. Does the section Love, Sex and Youth Work seem accurate to you? If not, why? If so, think of ways to avoid the pitfalls described in Ron's story and to overcome the tendency toward inappropriate relationships described on page 170.

7. Would you describe yourself as a walking wounded or a wounded healer? How does this affect your ministry?

Endnotes

[1]Stephen Apthorp, "Drug Abuse and the Church: Are the Blind Leading the Blind?" The Christian CENTURY (November 9, 1988), 1010.

[2]Gordon MacDonald, *Ordering Your Private World* (Nashville, TN: Thomas Nelson, 1984), 48-51.

[3]Dr. John F. Flora, "ACoA Clergy" (a letter to the editor), Changes, (January/February 1988), 77-78.

[4]Apthorp, "Drug Abuse and the Church: Are the Blind Leading the Blind?" 1010.

[5]Henri Nouwen, *The Wounded Healer: Ministry in Contemporary Society* (Garden City, NY: Doubleday, 1979).

Wishes, Dreams and Hopes

To close this book, I have a wish, a dream and a hope. And these lead me to a challenge.

A Wish

My wish is to relive my teenage and young adult years with all the understanding I now have as a child of an alcoholic. I don't wish for a whole new life or even a new family without an alcoholic parent. Either would require sacrificing memories and people I cherish. Instead, I wish I could replay those years without replaying the role or living by the rules that controlled my life.

If my wish would come true, I believe:

● I wouldn't have led two lives—one of professional success, the other of haunting personal failure.

● I would've known sooner that loving my wife and child involves much more than being a good provider.

● I would've been less compulsive and more intentional in my work—saying no much more often than I've said yes.

● I wouldn't have emotionally neglected—even abandoned—the ones I profess to love the most.

● I would've fulfilled my dreams instead of living my destiny.

But in the real world, wishes rarely come true—especially those that involve changing the past. So, little by little, day by day, I let go of the wish in order to face life as it was and is. I grieve the pain, the lost opportunities, the broken dreams and the consequences of my own birthright of dysfunction. And, finally, I forgive.

A Dream

My dream is that no more children anywhere will grow into adulthood to live out a destiny of pain they've inherited from their alcoholic families.

Sadly, dreams are only slightly more probable than wishes. Certainly, this dream won't be fulfilled in the near future.

But the great thing about dreams is that they become goals.

This book represents a small step toward my goal. Yet this small step will be stretched significantly if:

● It helps you become more sensitive to the special needs of kids growing up with alcoholic parents.

● It teaches you to give Healthy Help more often than Nice Help.

● It moves your church and group toward the goal of being a nurturing family model for wounded people.

● It encourages you to join the company of wounded healers.

● It empowers you to reach out with a message of hope to at least one victim of parental alcoholism.

And that brings me to my hope.

A Hope

My hope is that this book will make a difference in your ministry to at least one teenage child of an alcoholic. If it does, then it has been worth the time, energy and even the emotional pain I've invested in it.

When your ministry touches one teenager who's living

in an alcoholic home, it can give that teenager hope:

- hope that life can change;
- hope that he or she doesn't have to follow the dysfunctional rules and roles inherited from parents;
- hope that the future can be better than the past; and
- hope that God's healing hand can work in his or her life, with the grace, freedom and fullness of the abundant life Christ died to give.

A Challenge

In this book, I've tried to give you a basic understanding of the effects of growing up in an alcoholic family. I've written specifically to church youth workers because I believe you have so much to offer teenagers from alcoholic families.

But no matter what tools I give you in this book, none of them is sufficient to make you a Healthy Helper for kids from alcoholic families. Healthy Help is so much more than the things we do. It is who and what we are.

If you are genuine, caring, straightforward, trustworthy and loving, then the help that flows from you will be of the healthiest kind. When you add to this help the practical knowledge and ideas from this book, I think you'll be able to minister effectively to victims of alcoholism.

This is my challenge and prayer for you: May you live and minister in the name of Jesus Christ in such a way that gives Healthy Help and empowers children of alcoholics to claim their blessing of God's grace and love.

Appendixes

When a Parent Drinks Too Much

A COA Awareness Meeting

I f you have 20 to 25 kids in your youth group, you could have four to six group members from alcoholic families. You may not know about the alcoholism in their families. In fact, the teenagers themselves may not realize the negative impact their families have on them.

This meeting raises awareness about living in an alcoholic family. It helps teenagers from alcoholic families begin to recognize their own needs. And it helps other group members grow more sensitive to their peers who may live in dysfunctional families.

Objectives

In this meeting, group members will:
- experience how people wear masks to hide things;
- learn about roles kids play in alcoholic families;
- participate in a melodrama that explores the dynamics of a dysfunctional family;
- discover that they can break free of destructive roles with God's help; and

● offer to God one "mask" they wear, who can heal the pain behind the mask.

Preparation

Before you lead this meeting, read this book. Unless you understand the dynamics of alcoholic families, you could actually hurt group members in such families.

For the meeting, gather:

● Punch, plastic champagne glasses and inexpensive hors d'oeuvres (such as crackers, cookies, nuts and raw vegetables) to serve during the Mask Masquerade

● Construction paper, scissors, string and markers—or old magazines and paste—to make masks

● Chairs, arranged in a circle

● One copy of each section of the "Real-Life Stories" handout

● Seven posterboard signs, each showing a different symbol in "The Castle of Secrets" story

● Newsprint and markers

● A pencil or pen for each group member

● One sheet of newsprint with the "Serenity Prayer" written on it:

> God, grant me the serenity
> To accept the things I cannot change,
> The courage to change the things I can,
> And the wisdom to know the difference.

● A song and someone to accompany it on piano or guitar during the Removal of the Masks activity

● An offering plate or basket to collect the masks, or matches to burn the masks

● Optional: Order copies of the Children of Alcoholics Screening Test for each group member. See resources on page 198 for the address. For a sample, see page 114.

Mask Masquerade

Create a setting like a celebrity cocktail party. Serve

punch in plastic champagne glasses, and have a variety of inexpensive hors d'oeuvres.

As kids arrive, have them each make a construction paper mask to represent someone famous they'd like to be like. Do this one of two ways:

● Have kids use different shapes of masks and different colors to represent different famous people. Have each group member write the famous person's name on his or her mask's forehead.

● Have kids cut out simple masks. Then have each group member paste a magazine picture of the famous person on his or her mask.

Have them use string to put the masks on. Then have them join the celebrity party and each try to act like the person on their mask. They can introduce themselves to each other and tell stories about their great exploits. For example, if a teenager chooses a rock star, he or she can tell about working on a new album, the upcoming concert tour, singing at the White House or living in Hollywood.

When everyone has had about five minutes to mingle, have the group sit in a circle.

Ask each person:

● **Why did you choose the person you chose? What characteristics do you admire in that person?**

● **Do you think you're actually a lot like the person or quite different? Explain.**

● **How did it feel to try to act like another person? Was it fun, confusing, freeing, frustrating? Give examples.**

● **When do you feel you wear "masks" in real life? Why do you wear them? What do you want to hide when you wear your masks?**

Then say: **We all wear masks sometimes. But some people wear masks all the time. They get so used to wearing their masks that they forget who they really are.**

We're going to focus on one group like this today: teenagers from alcoholic families. You probably don't

recognize these people because their masks look so real and so "together." They may not even recognize themselves. But behind the masks is a lot of deep pain that can affect the rest of their lives if they don't recognize it and take off their masks.

Have kids keep their masks.

A Look Behind the Masks

Divide your group into four teams. Give each team a different case study section from the "Real-Life Stories" handout on pages 193-196. Explain that the four different stories tell about brothers and sisters in one family. Ask kids in each team to read the story aloud, answer the questions and be ready to report to the whole group on what they've learned.

Give about five minutes for discussion. Then bring the group together and have teams share their reports. Then discuss the relationships between these brothers and sisters. Which relationships do you think are strong and which ones are weak?

"The Castle of Secrets" Melodrama

Say: **Alcoholism is a widespread problem that's often hard to see. But how does it affect family members? Let's explore what it's like to live in an alcoholic family. We'll focus on three "rules" in alcoholic families that can make life extremely difficult for everyone—especially the kids.**

Then say you're going to read a melodrama to the group. Explain what you want the group to do when a volunteer holds up different signs:

: Smile and cup your hands around your face like sunshine.

: Snap your fingers.

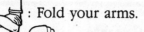 : Fold your arms.

: Flex your biceps.

: Cover your mouth with your hand.

: Scratch your head.

: Cup your hands over your head to represent a light bulb.

Ask a volunteer to hold up the signs as they're indicated in the right column. Have kids practice each action with the signs. Then read "The Castle of Secrets" story (pages 186-188).

After the melodrama, ask:
● **When in the melodrama did you realize something might be wrong in the Palace of Sincerity?**
● **What feelings did you have as I read the story?**
● **When did you feel the boy's situation was the best? the worst? Explain your answer.**
● **Why do you think the Keepers wouldn't tell the boy the Great Lie?**
● **Why did they get so angry with the boy when he discovered the Great Lie?**
● **Do you think the boy made the right choice when he pledged not to talk, trust and feel? Why or why not?**
● **What do you think life will be like for the boy in the Palace of Sincerity?**
● **Do you think the boy will ever leave the Palace of Sincerity? Why or why not?**
● **What would it take for the boy to leave?**
Help the group members make connections between the melodrama and life in an alcoholic family. Explain that these families have three rules—"don't talk," "don't trust," "don't feel"—that make life difficult and painful. The families deny their problem and become angry at anyone who

The Castle of Secrets

Story	Sign
Once there was a bright and precocious boy. The boy lived in an extraordinary place called the Palace of Sincerity. He lived there with a group of people known as the Keepers of the Lie.	
His earliest years were pleasant and fun. He enjoyed being with the Keepers of the Lie because of the fabulous stories they created and told. But as the boy grew older, he became uncomfortable. He couldn't be sure when—or even if—the Keepers of the Lie were being truthful. This bothered him.	
One day, as the boy thought about his life in the Palace of Sincerity, an idea burst into his mind. He wondered why the Keepers would never tell him the Great Lie. Each time he asked they'd tell him a different answer. So he was pretty sure they never really told him.	
Then, suddenly, he understood. He knew the Great Lie! The Great Lie, he reasoned, was about the Palace of Sincerity: It wasn't really the Palace of Sincerity; it was the Castle of Secrets!	
Though the boy was overjoyed at last to know the Great Lie, he felt even more uncomfortable. He couldn't understand why the Keepers of the Lie wouldn't admit where they lived. Perhaps they didn't know. He decided to tell them.	
At the first mention of the name "Castle of Secrets" the Keepers of the Lie became very upset. They denied they lived in the Castle. It was truly the Palace, they asserted. They quizzed the boy about how he could get such an idea. In wails and sobs, they asked how he could call his wonderful home the Castle of Secrets. The boy had never	

continued

seen the Keepers of the Lie carry on so!

Just as suddenly as their tirade started, it stopped. The Keepers huddled in the corner. After several minutes of whispering and hushing, they calmly walked back to the boy, each wearing a Cheshire-cat-like smile. For the next few minutes they talked with him about their good life together. They told him what a fine young man he had become. Finally they asked if he'd like to become, with them, a Keeper of the Lie.

Though all encouraged the boy to join their alliance, a tiny voice inside him told him to beware. After several minutes of excited pleadings he told them he couldn't become one of them. He couldn't be a Keeper of the Lie.

From that time on, life in the Castle of Secrets changed. No longer did the Keepers tell the boy fantastic stories. They didn't even include him in conversations. And when they did, the conversation was forced and insincere. When the boy went into a room, the Keepers would fall silent. Then they'd only talk in low murmurs among themselves.

The boy's life became unbearable. He wondered what he should do. He mulled over his options. He wouldn't become a Keeper. He was too young to leave the Castle of Secrets. Besides, he'd never been outside the Castle. The Keepers of the Lie might know the way out—though he couldn't be sure. But they surely wouldn't let him leave now that he knew their Great Lie.

A cruel chill came over the boy as he realized his plight. He knew how it must feel to be one of the fireflies he sometimes captured in a jar on a summer evening. They would eventually die because the jar was tightly closed. Even though the boy tried to make the jar "home" for the insect friends, they still died. Like those bugs, he felt des-

continued

tined to suffocate in his artificial world.

No! No! He wouldn't die! There was another way. Someday he'd be old enough to find the way out of the Castle—to leave forever. All he had to do was survive and escape.

But how?

First, he thought, if the Keepers didn't want to talk to him, that would be fine. He'd stop talking to them too. That would keep the peace.

Next, he wouldn't be dependent on them anymore. He was living only to get out, so he needed to become independent anyway. Why not start now?

Finally, he wouldn't allow himself to be bothered by the Keepers' rejection any longer. If they wanted to be that way, fine. But it wasn't going to bother him—at least, he'd never let them know he was bothered.

With his new plan, the boy branded his threefold commitment on his heart. He pledged he wouldn't talk, trust or feel. These safeguards, he knew, would help him survive and even escape. Once out, he'd establish his own home free of secrets and lies—especially the Great Lie. It would be nothing like the Castle of Secrets.

What the boy couldn't know was that he became a Keeper of the Lie that day. His pledges were the same ones everyone else in the Castle had made in their own time and way as they had also discovered the Great Lie.

The boy, now grown up, lives in a place he calls the Pavilion of Truth.

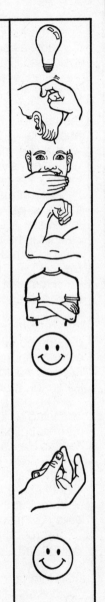

suggests they even have a problem.

Ask:

● **How does it feel when you can't talk to people about your problems or important things?**

● **What's it like to be with someone who seems calloused and emotionless?**

● **When do you feel you follow the rules of alcoholic families?** (Explain to the group that we all live with these kinds of rules sometimes. That's normal. But the rules are in force all the time in alcoholic families.)

● **How can other people help someone who feels he or she has to live by these rules?**

Life Without Masks

Say: **The boy in the melodrama felt helpless. He didn't see any way out of the Castle of Secrets, and he didn't feel any hope. So he gave up. But as Christians we know that there is a way out. Christ sets us free of the rules that keep us from experiencing abundant life.**

Then read aloud 2 Corinthians 5:17: **"Therefore, if anyone is in Christ, he is a new creation; the old has gone, the new has come!"**

On newsprint, draw a two-column chart. Label one side "Old" and the other side "New." Ask kids to think of things that happen in alcoholic families related to the rules and masks. List these in the Old column. Then ask how Christ can change each of these old things into something new. List these in the New column. For example, "secrets" can change into "honesty." Or "don't feel" can become "vulnerability."

Removal of the Masks

Give each person a pencil or pen. Ask kids each to write on his or her mask one mask he or she wears. For example, kids may write, "I always act like everything's okay, even when I feel lousy." Assure kids that no one will know what they write. It will be kept confidential.

After everyone has finished, say: **When alcoholics and their families begin to heal, the first thing they learn is that they're powerless over the problem. They have to give it to God—the only one who has the power to heal our wounds and change our lives. Tonight we're going to give our masks to God, and ask him to teach us to live honestly and openly without masks.**

Pass around an offering plate, or place one in the middle of the circle. Ask group members to place their masks in the plate. Assure them that you'll destroy the masks immediately after the meeting. No one will read them.

While you're collecting the mask offering, have the group sing a song such as "Come to the Water," "Amazing Grace" or "Just as I Am" (in *Songs*, Songs and Creations Inc.).

If you have a fireplace or can easily go outside where it's safe, have kids toss their masks into the fire instead of collecting them.

The "Serenity Prayer"

Say: **The "Serenity Prayer" is important to many recovering victims of alcoholism—spouses, children and alcoholics themselves. It's frequently used to open support group meetings, such as Alcoholics Anonymous, Al-Anon and Alateen. Today we'll use it to close our meeting. But between each line of the prayer, I'll explain it a little.**

Post the newsprint that shows the "Serenity Prayer." Have the group form a circle and hold hands. Lead the group to read aloud each line, and add comments between each line as follows:

GOD, GRANT ME THE SERENITY TO ACCEPT THE THINGS I CANNOT CHANGE,

Among the things you can't change is your family. This is true whether your family is alcoholic or not.

You just can't change other people, no matter how much you want to help them.

THE COURAGE TO CHANGE THE THINGS I CAN,

You can only change yourself. The first step is to change the rules you live by. You can choose to break unhealthy family rules by admitting the hurt and fear you feel. Take a risk and tell someone you trust about your problem. You help your family best when you help yourself first. It takes a lot of courage, but God can give you the strength.

AND THE WISDOM TO KNOW THE DIFFERENCE.

It's not always easy to know what we can and can't change. The Bible tells us: "If any of you lacks wisdom, he should ask God, who gives generously to all without finding fault, and it will be given to him" (James 1:5). God will help us discern the truth when we feel confused.

Then recite the "Serenity Prayer" together without interruption. End the meeting with hugs or with some other appropriate physical touches for affirmation.

If you didn't burn the masks, immediately destroy them after the meeting. Do not under any circumstance break group members' confidence by looking at the masks. Encourage kids to come talk with you individually, now or later, if they want to talk about their own situations at home.

Optional Activities

● Show a film about alcoholic families instead of doing the melodrama. Two good films:

1. *Children of Denial*—a 28-minute film with COA expert Dr. Claudia Black describing the effects of the three rules on kids in alcoholic families. (Available from A.C.T., Box 8536, Newport Beach, CA 92660.)

2. *Soft Is the Heart of a Child*—a 30-minute dramatic presentation of alcoholism's impact on the family's children. (Available from Gerald T. Rogers Productions, 5225 Old Or-

chard Rd., Suite 6, Skokie, IL 60077.)

● In place of the melodrama, invite a recovering child of an alcoholic to speak to your group about his or her family rules and the experiences of growing up in an alcoholic family. Local Alateen or Adult Children of Alcoholics chapters can often suggest appropriate speakers.

● Give the Children of Alcoholics Screening Test (page 114) after the melodrama discussion. At a later time tabulate the results and talk individually with teenagers who appear to be from alcoholic families. Order multiple copies of the test from the address in the resource listing on page 198.

Real-Life Stories

Marti

Marti, 17, is the oldest of four children. Her dad, who owns a small business, is an alcoholic. Her mom works outside the home to supplement the family's modest income.

Marti worries a lot. She worries that her dad drinks too much—though she doesn't believe he's an alcoholic. She worries about her mother, because she always seems to be working so hard. And she worries for her brothers and sisters.

Since Dad spends so much time drinking with his friends and Mom is always working, Marti does a lot of household chores. She's also the one who hears everyone's problems—including her parents'. In many ways, she's like a little mom to everyone.

Marti is quite involved in her church. She's an active youth group member—president, in fact. While she likes the feeling of being president, she frequently feels frustrated because it seems no one is as committed to the group as she is.

That feeling of being overwhelmed by responsibility and frustrated that no one else seems to do as much is a part of life as a Family Hero.

1. Why do you think Marti is called a Family Hero?

2. What do you think she hopes to accomplish by being a Family Hero?

3. If you met Marti at school or church, would you suspect she's from an alcoholic family? Why or why not?

4. If you were Marti's friend, how would you respond to her? Explain.

Mark

Mark, 16, is the second oldest of four children. His dad owns his own business and is an alcoholic. His mom works to make things a little easier for the family.

Mark has pretty well written off his family. He feels alienated, so he spends as much time away from the family as he can. He feels blamed for the family's problems. Family members have even told him so—particularly his oldest sister, who he calls "Sister Saintly."

Mark isn't into school. He goes, but that's about it. He tried out for the basketball team last year, but the coach gave him a lecture on the first day. "Look, kid," the coach said. "You're welcome to try out for the team, but I have a warning for you. I've talked with your folks, so I know some of the junk you put them through. I won't stand for that kind of stuff around here. The first time you mess up, you're out." Mark finished his tryout, but didn't even go back the next day to see the results.

Mark doesn't bother with church either, even though his family attends regularly. He hates to dress up and act like the family's so perfect. He does go to church on religious holidays. But even that's tough, since all those elderly women tell him they're praying for him. Actually, Mark wouldn't mind if they prayed, if they'd stop telling him about it.

After all, when you're the Scapegoat of the family, you really do need a lot of prayer just to survive.

1. Why do you think Mark is called a Scapegoat?

2. For Mark, what are the benefits of being the Scapegoat? the problems?

3. If you met Mark at school or church, would you suspect he's from an alcoholic family? Why or why not?

4. If you were Mark's friend, how would you respond to him? Explain.

Todd

Todd, 15, is the second youngest of four children. His dad, an alcoholic, owns a small business. His mom works a night job to help the family get by.

Todd is extremely talented. He can make people laugh at just about anything. Everyone tells him he should be a professional comedian or clown, because he has a way of making people feel better when they're down. Even more, he has a real gift for timing; he knows just when everyone needs a good laugh. And everyone seems to appreciate it.

Well, almost everyone.

Todd likes school, though he doesn't get good grades. He dreads parent-teacher conferences, because the same thing always comes up: "Todd is a fine young man with lots of potential. The only thing standing in his way is his mouth. He's got a great sense of humor, but he chooses the worst times to use it."

Unlike his older brother, Todd goes to church. Like most things, he doesn't take it too seriously. But it has its moments. He goes to youth group too, but not for spiritual reasons. He likes to see his sister, the youth group president, get frustrated trying to make him be serious.

A lot of people like Todd, but he doesn't have many close friends. In fact, he can't think of one. Being the family Mascot, you'd think he'd know how to cheer himself up. But it's not so easy when the sadness is within you.

1. Why do you think Todd is called a Mascot?

2. What do you think Todd hopes to do by keeping everyone around him laughing?

3. If you met Todd at school or church, would you suspect he's from an alcoholic family? Why or why not?

4. If you were Todd's friend, how would you respond to him? Explain.

Lindy

Lindy, 13, is the youngest of four children. Her dad, an alcoholic, is a self-employed business operator. Her mom works outside the home too, but Lindy wishes she were around more.

Everyone tells Lindy she's a "really sweet kid," yet she's not sure it's true. If it were true, she reasons, why doesn't anyone want to spend more time with her? Lindy feels lonely and abandoned most of the time—even with two brothers and a sister.

Lindy doesn't really care for school. She'd rather spend her time listening to music or watching television. She feels embarrassed around other kids because of her weight. Sometimes they call her names, and she just runs to the bathroom and cries.

Lindy does like church, though. She especially likes the times of quiet prayer and soft singing in the Sunday services. She goes to youth group because her older sister, the youth group president, wants her to be involved.

Not many places are comfortable for Lindy—not even her home. When her folks fight, which is often, she doesn't know what to do. Part of her wants to run, and another part wants to make everything better for her mom and dad. But all she can do is get out of the way—just like a good Lost Child.

1. Why do you think Lindy is called a Lost Child?

2. What do you think Lindy hopes will happen when she stays out of everyone's way and doesn't cause problems?

3. If you met Lindy at school or church, would you suspect she's from an alcoholic family?

4. If you were Lindy's friend, how would you respond to her? Explain.

Recommended Resources

Books and Pamphlets

The following resources represent some of the best available material on alcoholism and children of alcoholics. Many of the books are available at local bookstores. Or you can order them from the publisher.

Adult Children of Alcoholics. Janet Geringer Woititz. Health Communications, 1721 Blount Rd., Ste. 1, Pompano Beach, FL 33069. Describes the problems facing adult children of alcoholics and suggests ways to solve the problems. A national best seller.

Alcoholics Anonymous. Alcoholics Anonymous World Services, Box 459, Grand Central Station, New York, NY 10163. Serves as the basic recovery manual and sourcebook for alcoholics. Has been revised several times since it was first written by AA's founder, Bill Wilson.

Alcoholism: A Merry-Go-Round Named Denial. Joseph Kellermann. Hazelden Educational Materials, Pleasant Valley Rd., Box 176, Center City, MN 55012. Details the dynamics of alcoholic families.

Bradshaw On: The Family. John Bradshaw. Health Communications, 1721 Blount Rd., Ste. 1, Pompano Beach, FL 33069. Examines—in clear, understandable terms—family dynamics from a family-systems perspective.

Broken Bottles, Broken Dreams: Understanding and Helping Children of Alcoholics. Charles Deutsch. Teachers College Press, 1234 Amsterdam Ave., New York, NY 10027. Describes in detail Massachusetts' CASPAR project, which intervenes to help school-age children of alcoholics.

Chemical Dependency Treatment Programs: A Guide to Referral. Will Maloney. Hazelden Educational Materials, Pleasant Valley Rd., Box 176, Center City, MN 55012. Provides basic guidelines for making informed referrals.

Children of Alcoholics: A Bibliography and Resource Guide. Robert Ackerman. Health Communications, 1721 Blount Rd., Ste. 1, Pompano Beach, FL 33069. Supplies an exhaustive annotated list of films, audio/video cassettes, books and other resources that address COA concerns. Should be on the shelf of everyone who's serious about helping children of alcoholics.

Children of Alcoholics Screening Test and Test Manual. Dr. John W. Jones. Camelot Unlimited, 5 N. Wabash Ave., Ste. 1409, Chicago, IL 60602. Includes multiple copies of the Children of Alcoholics Screening Test, plus detailed reliability studies, case studies, and instructions for administering, scoring and interpreting the test.

Christian Ministry and the Fifth Step. Edward Sellner. Hazelden Educational Materials, Pleasant Valley Rd., Box 176, Center City, MN 55012. Describes the minister's function and responsibilities as a Fifth Step listener in the 12-Step recovery process.

Co-Dependence: Misunderstood-Mistreated. Anne Wilson Schaef. Winston Press, 600 First Ave. North, Minneapolis, MN 55403. Explains co-dependence as part of the addictive process. A best-selling, foundational book.

Counseling Teenagers. G. Keith Olson. Group Books, Box 481, Loveland, CO 80539. Supplies youth workers a basic text to use in counseling teenagers with a variety of problems and concerns, including alcohol abuse.

Drugs, God and Me. Kathleen Hamilton Eschner and Nancy G. Nelson. Group Books, Box 481, Loveland, CO

80539. Provides a unique curriculum resource for junior highers and their parents, focusing on alcohol and drug abuse prevention.

The Encyclopedia of Alcoholism. Robert O'Brien and Morris Chafetz. Facts on File Publications, 460 Park Ave., South, New York, NY 10016. Outlines basic information about alcoholism in a dictionary format.

Free to Know, Free to Choose. Hazelden Educational Materials, Pleasant Valley Rd., Box 176, Center City, MN 55012. Aids Christian educators in drug and alcohol awareness classes.

Generation to Generation. Edwin Friedman. Guilford Press, 200 Park Ave. South, New York, NY 10003. Helps understand the church as a family—both at its functional best and dysfunctional worst.

It Will Never Happen to Me! Claudia Black. M.A.C. Communications, 1850 High St., Denver, CO 80218. Explains alcoholic family rules and COA roles. A standard.

The Journey of the Beatitudes. Richard Wilson. Hazelden Educational Materials, Pleasant Valley Rd., Box 176, Center City, MN 55012. Compares the 12 Steps with Jesus' teachings in the Beatitudes.

Lost in the Shuffle: The Co-Dependent Reality. Robert Subby. Health Communications, 1721 Blount Rd., Ste. 1, Pompano Beach, FL 33069. Examines facets of codependency as it relates to several types of troubled family systems.

Pastoral Care for Alcoholism: An Introduction. Conrad Bergendoff. Hazelden Educational Materials, Pleasant Valley Rd., Box 176, Center City, MN 55012. Deals with the pastor's role in helping alcoholics and their families.

Preparing Your Church for Ministry to Alcoholics and Their Families. Thomas Hamilton Cairns. Charles C. Thomas Publisher, 2600 South First St., Springfield, IL 62708. Examines the church's role in ministering to alcoholics and their families, and suggests a specific model and standards for such a ministry.

Providing Care for Children of Alcoholics. David Lewis

and Carol Williams (editors). Health Communications, 1721 Blount Rd., Ste. 1, Pompano Beach, FL 33069. Features a series of articles on helping children of alcoholics.

The Secret Everyone Knows. Cathleen Brooks. Operation Cork, 8939 Villa La Jolla Dr., Ste. 203, San Diego, CA 92037. Describes life for teenage children of alcoholics, as well as options for receiving help.

Sin: Overcoming the Ultimate Deadly Addiction. J. Keith Miller. Harper & Row, Publishers, 10 East 53rd St., New York, NY 10022. Examines sin as an addiction. A helpful explanation of addiction.

A Straight Word to Kids and Parents. Hutterian Brethren (editors). Plough Publishing House, Ulster Park, NY 12487. Addresses a number of potential teenage problems, including living with alcoholic parents.

A Teenager's Guide to Living With an Alcoholic Parent. Edith Hornik-Beer. Hazelden Educational Materials, Pleasant Valley Rd., Box 176, Center City, MN 55012. Answers teenagers' questions about alcoholism and situations that arise in an alcoholic home. Offers straightforward guidance.

Traits of a Healthy Family. Dolores Curran. Ballantine Books, 201 East 50th St., New York, NY 10022. Identifies the basic components of healthy family life.

Victims No More. Thomas McCabe. Hazelden Educational Materials, Pleasant Valley Rd., Box 176, Center City, MN 55012. Describes how the family system changes to accommodate alcoholism, confront it and eventually move it into recovery.

When Your Parent Drinks Too Much: A Book for Teenagers. Eric Ryerson. Facts on File Publications, 460 Park Ave., South, New York, NY 10016. Discusses alcoholism and its effects on the family. Suggests appropriate ways for teenagers to respond to an alcoholic parent.

Organizations

The following organizations are provided as "seed" for your own reference and referral files. Many publish helpful materials, and will assist in contacting services and professionals in your own community.

Adult Children of Alcoholics, 6381 Hollywood Blvd., Ste. 685, Hollywood, CA 90028. Organizes support groups for adult children of alcoholics. One of the fastest-growing self-help support systems in the United States.

Al-Anon/Alateen Family Group Headquarters, Box 862, Midtown Station, New York, NY 10018. Provides information about support groups for family members from alcoholic families. The headquarters for the 12-Step support groups.

Alcoholics Anonymous, Box 459, Grand Central Station, New York, NY 10163. Helps alcoholics through the recovery process with its 12-Step program.

Children Are People, 493 Selby Ave., St. Paul, MN 55102. Helps young children of alcoholics.

Do It Now Foundation, 2050 East University Dr., Phoenix, AZ 85034. Publishes numerous fine resources to build awareness of alcohol addiction and other chemical dependencies.

Hazelden Educational Materials, Pleasant Valley Rd., Box 176, Center City, MN 55012. Offers numerous continuing education opportunities. One of the leading publishers of addictions-education materials using the 12-Step approach.

Health Communications, 1721 Blount Rd., Ste. 1, Pompano Beach, FL 33069. Publishes numerous books and resources for children of alcoholic families.

National Association for Children of Alcoholics, 13706 Coast Hwy., Ste. 201, South Laguna, CA 92677. Co-produces (with the National Committee for Prevention of Child Abuse) packets on alcoholic families featuring Marvel comic's heroes.

National Council on Alcoholism, 12 West 21st St., 7th Floor, New York, NY 10010. Provides resources, research and other information about alcoholism.

Strengthen Your Youth Ministry

MINISTRY TO FAMILIES WITH TEENAGERS
By Dub Ambrose and Walt Mueller

Increase your youth ministry's impact by offering practical strategies for supporting and nurturing your teenagers' families. You'll get sound programming ideas to . . .
- Help parents understand their kids
- Improve parent/teenager communication
- Help families deal with conflict
- Determine the needs of parents and their young people
- Involve parents as youth ministry volunteers

Unlock the potential for strong families in your church. **Ministry to Families With Teenagers** will equip you with guidance, encouragement and tools for reaching teenagers where they're affected the most—in their families.

ISBN 0-931529-54-9 $16.95

COUNSELING TEENAGERS
By Dr. G. Keith Olson

Get in-depth and timely insight on counseling adolescents. You'll . . .
- Understand how teenagers develop physically and emotionally
- Gain insight for helping your young people
- Learn about counseling skills and techniques
- Understand the powerful role of the family on teenage development
- Approach counseling as a Christian

Order your copy of this comprehensive and intentionally Christian reference for understanding and helping your young people today.

Paperback   ISBN 0-931529-67-0 $14.95
Hardcover   ISBN 0936-664-15-0 $19.95

BEATING BURNOUT IN YOUTH MINISTRY
By Dean Feldmeyer

Fight burnout, get more done, and still have time for your family and yourself. With this easy-to-read guide you'll discover practical, new ways to:
- Set realistic goals
- Eliminate time-wasters
- Learn when and how to say no
- Find time to recharge your creative batteries

Plus, you'll get helpful worksheets, revealing self-quizzes and loads of practical insights for both novices and pros. Take control of your schedule today with **Beating Burnout in Youth Ministry.**

ISBN 0-931529-47-6 $9.95

More Ministry Building Resources

THE YOUTH MINISTRY RESOURCE BOOK
Edited by Eugene C. Roehlkepartain

Stay on top of youth ministry, young people and their world with the most complete, reliable and up-to-date resource book ever!
- Get the facts on today's teenagers
- Find out who's doing what in youth ministry
- Get the scoop on youth ministry salaries
- Discover resources galore!

Depend on **The Youth Ministry Resource Book** to help you plan youth meetings and retreats. Write newsletters. Prepare youth talks and sermons. Work with parents of teenagers and more. You'll find support for your ministry to young people with this handy gold mine of information.

ISBN 0-931529-22-0 $16.95

BUILDING ATTENDANCE IN YOUR YOUTH MINISTRY
By Scott C. Noon

Now you can make your group grow—and learn what to do when it does! You'll get practical ideas for bringing new kids in the door, and design faith-building programs to keep them coming back. Discover . . .
- Formulas for setting realistic goals
- Hints for planning long-term expansion
- Effective ways to handle growth

Whether you're just starting out or a youth ministry veteran, you'll get tools that really work—for building attendance in *your* youth group!

ISBN 0-931529-84-0 $10.95

FAST FORMS FOR YOUTH MINISTRY
Compiled by Lee Sparks

Here's a lifesaver for busy youth workers. **Fast Forms for Youth Ministry** gives you 70 ready-to-copy forms, schedules, checklists and letters to save you time and effort. In just minutes, you'll have ready-to-use documents that took hours to produce and perfect. Each form is designed to help you better organize and manage your ministry.

Make your ministry more effective with this practical, useful tool.

ISBN 0-931529-25-5 $11.95

Creative Resources for Your Youth Ministry

10-MINUTE DEVOTIONS FOR YOUTH GROUPS
By J.B. Collingsworth

Get this big collection of ready-to-use devotion ideas that'll help teenagers apply God's Word to their lives. Each 10-minute faith-building devotion addresses an important concern such as:
- love
- failure
- faith, and more
- peer pressure
- rejection

You'll get 52 quick devotions complete with scripture reference, attention-grabbing learning experience, discussion questions and a closing. Bring teenagers closer to God with these refreshing devotions—perfect for youth activities of any kind!

ISBN 0-931529-85-9 $6.95

QUICK SKITS & DISCUSSION STARTERS
By Chuck Bolte and Paul McCusker

Here's a new tool for grabbing attention and building faith in youth groups. Help your teenagers build confidence and self-esteem. Improve communication skills. Practice teamwork. And examine issues from a Christian perspective. You'll get complete instructions, 26 simple warm-up exercises, 18 quick skits and thought-provoking discussion questions with matching biblical references.

ISBN 0-931529-68-9 $9.95

YOUTH-LED MEETINGS, VOL. 1
By Dr. Elaine Clanton Harpine

Offer your young people the opportunity to develop important leadership skills by accepting responsibility. Making decisions. Working with others, and more. You'll see group attendance increase as teenagers become more involved with their group.

Discover 10 creative, biblically-based meeting plans with step-by-step instructions that teenagers can lead themselves. Plus, you'll get everything you need to successfully guide your group through youth-led meetings.

ISBN 0-931529-53-0 $12.95

These and other Group products are available at your local Christian bookstore. Or order direct from the publisher. Write Group, Box 481, Loveland, CO 80539. Please add $2.50 for postage and handling. Colorado residents add 3% sales tax.